Subsidiarity

A Quick Reference Guide

Subsidiarity: a Negative Form

"It is an injustice, a grave evil and a disturbance of right order for a larger and higher organization to arrogate to itself functions which can be performed efficiently by smaller and lower bodies."

Pius XI, *Quadragesimo Anno* (1931)

Subsidiarity: a Positive Form

"A community of a higher order ... should support a community of a lower order in case of need and help to coordinate its activity with the activities of the rest of society, always with a view to the common good."

John Paul II, *Centesimus Annus* (1991)

Subsidiarity in ten words or less

"Let's not make a Federal case out of this."

(an American epigram)

The Golden Rule of Subsidiarity

"Be as ready to assist others
as you would want them
to be ready to assist you."

Subsidiarity

Peter J. Floriani, Ph.D.

Penn Street Productions
Reading, PA

The cover photo shows the famous "big dish" by which file transport
via satellite to remote locations was performed
on a daily basis between March 2, 2000 and August 31, 2005.

The software which was used has long since vanished into the dim past,
but the principle of Subsidiarity remains as valid and as powerful as ever.

For more information, visit

http://DeBellisStellarum/Subsidiarity

Produced by

Penn Street Productions,
Reading, PA

ISBN-13 978-1480237544
ISBN-10 148023754X

Dedication

Ad Majorem Dei Gloriam

and to

Mary, the Gate of Heaven

"You are the *Portal* to life immortal..."
"Guide us *Home*-ward, Oh Mary!"

In Memoriam

Leo XIII
Pius XI
John XXIII
Paul VI
John Paul II

With special thanks to

Joe Kovach
Diane Michael
Joe Peleggi

and the specialists of
Traffic, the Tech Shop, the Field Techs,
and especially the Control Room Operators.

Table of Contents

Preface

Dr. Floriani was able to apply the theory of subsidiarity to the communications field to reduce our workflow to its simplest and most efficient means. He found solutions to technical problems in the most unexpected places, and they were always effective.

Joe Kovach

Foreword

This story began on March 2, 2000, and went on for 2000 days. Some 200,000 spots were encoded. Over 150 inserters were built and installed and maintained at over 60 headends. Every day some 200 schedules were sent, and 4000 logs were retrieved. And each day, *subsidiarity* was performed according to some 1200 portal spot requests, requiring the transport of about 120 spots.

Yes, subsidiarity. That was the term we used. Everyone knew that our spot transport machinery was called subsidiarity, and that it was invented by a Pope. They also knew that it was efficient: it did its job well – and when a new inserter was installed, they could watch it happening in the Control Room.

I was the one who wrote the code, the "man behind the curtain" – rather, behind the screens – the one who made the gears turn. Most of the time I sat around in the Control Room so I could WATCH everything run, but once in a while I got to push the buttons.

It's all over now, except for some wonderful friends, a handful of stories (including a full-length mystery novel called *Joe the Control Room Guy*), a poem or two, and some jokes. And this book – which, like Tolkien's story of the Sun and Moon in his *Silmarillion*, is the last radiant fruit of the system on which my co-workers and I worked so long to erect and maintain. This Tolkien reference is no meaningless allusion: the idea of the Tree is very important, as you will see. I am a Chestertonian as well as a computer scientist, and so my references may sometimes seem distant from my subject. But then, as Chesterton says, "I never can really feel that there is such a thing as a different subject."[1]

I have a number of people to thank. Rick Lugari, Nancy Brown, Sheila Jenné Connolly, Jim Waclawik, and Ann Putnam read versions of the book, and gave me useful suggestions for improvement. The completed work was also read by my spiritual director, Father Luke Anderson, O. Cist., who urged me to get it into print. Special thanks to Jim Homan, a professor at the Daniel J. Gross Catholic High School in Bellevue, Nebraska and his junior theology class of Spring 2009 who read portions of this book by means of the INTERNET, and in particular his student Katie P. who asked "What if I don't follow the rules of Subsidiarity?" It was their comments which led to a reworking of the part on Engineering, the chapter on Failure, and some additional material on Communications. Also to John and Sheila Connolly whose comments led to the inclusion of the chapter on extensions. Sheila also provided me with two additions to my study of the errors when Subsidiarity is violated; they arose in her actual experience, though I have found comparable cases to maintain a uniform presentation.

Finally, I express my deep gratitude to my good friends and co-workers, especially my boss, Joe Kovach, the Director of Operations; my counterpart from the Tech Shop, Joe Peleggi; our brilliant Traffic Director, Diane Michael; the people in Traffic, the Field Techs, and the Control Room guys, who made the system work.

Peter J. Floriani, Ph.D.

---

[1] GKC ILN Feb 17, 1906 CW27:126.

Part I
An Introduction To Subsidiarity

Chapter 1
Introduction

Whosoever is the greater among you, let him be your minister.
Mt 20:26
For I have received of the Lord that which also I delivered unto you...
1 Cor 11:23
Quidquid recipitur secundum modum recipientis recipitur.
Whatever is received is received according to the mode of the receiver.
"an ancient principle of knowledge" *Thomistic Metaphysics*, 19

The word "subsidiarity" is showing up more and more frequently in these days. Why? Because it is an important idea. Subsidiarity has been a major component of a special branch of philosophy called *Catholic Social Teaching* of the Roman Catholic Church for over a century – but for most of that time, it was thought to be merely an abstraction, or at best an ideal or example, which might be admired and even taught as a guiding principle, but was never really implemented. Or maybe thought not implementable at all.

Now that has changed. A large cable television company needed an efficient technique of delivering TV commercials in electronic form to a number of geographically distant sites. Machinery for transport and playback was designed and implemented, and the system performed its duties for more than five years, delivering over 100 commercials every day. It was precisely nothing less than subsidiarity turned into software. When the contract expired, the system was abandoned though it had been successful in accomplishing its goals. Indeed, the results we observed strongly urged a deeper consideration of the abstract idea.

This book, then, will describe the idea of Subsidiarity. After a short review of its history, I will present the cable TV spot transport problem, together with the solution we accomplished, thus providing a concrete analogy for discussion. Then I will consider some additional examples to extend, enrich, and apply the analogy, and conclude with some discussion of the relation of Subsidiarity to engineering.

What is Subsidiarity?

Subsidiarity is nothing more than common sense, as applied to the governance or control of an organization, or of collections (systems) of organizations. It is a simple idea, almost mathematical in tone, as it must be in order to have such vast application. Like other profound ideas, it can be expressed in a variety of forms, as it has been applied to the great variety of cases throughout history. The fundamental idea appeared at length in Leo XIII's 1891 encyclical, *Rerum Novarum*. Forty years later, Pius XI reduced it to a succinct but negative form:

It is an injustice, a grave evil and a disturbance of right order for a larger and higher organization to arrogate to itself functions which can be performed efficiently by smaller and lower bodies.

Quadragesimo Anno

In 1961, seventy years after Leo XIII, John XXIII called it the "principle of subsidiary function" which he simplified to "subsidiarity" in his 1963 *Pacem in Terris*. Perhaps the cleanest and most positive form is also one of the newest, formulated by John Paul II and appearing in 1991:

A community of a higher order ... should support a community of a lower order in case of need and help to coordinate its activity with the activities of the rest of society, always with a view to the common good.

Centesimus Annus 48

Subsidiarity is such an obvious idea that it is enshrined in witticisms such as "Keep it simple, stupid" and "Let's not make a federal case out of this." It is ancient: Moses used it, as we shall see when we explore its history. It is modern, being able to serve as the foundation of computer software for file transport by satellite, as I will demonstrate in detail.

Subsidiarity is also a paradox: it divides and also unites. Subsidiarity is setting forth one single task as a goal – as well as specifying separate functions or duties to be performed independently yet harmoniously, in order that the goal be achieved. When Subsidiarity is in effect, it produces that mystical inversion where the last shall be first and the first are last.[2]

It is not correct to say that Subsidiarity is *a way* as if it were merely one among many possible approaches – it actually is the *only way* to do things – or at least the only way which really has any hope of being practical, efficient, and result-producing. Though Subsidiarity is a general structure or strategy (it might be called a paradigm, or a "metarule") – and not a detailed and comprehensive specification, any given system will be more (or less) successful at its purposes to the extent it is in harmony (or dissonance) with Subsidiarity. And the larger and more complex a system is, the greater will be the need for Subsidiarity – and the more dreadful will be the failures for neglecting it.

As the term is generally used in documents of the Popes and social philosophy, Subsidiarity refers to strictly *human* organizations: families, businesses, trade unions, and the various forms of government from local to international – *as well as* all their varied interactions and contacts. Why is this? Because humans act according to *will*. And the human will is not ultimately subject to programming or control in the mechanical sense: it must be appealed to by truly powerful words like humility, duty and dedication, generosity, kindness and concern. Subsidiarity is a wide-scale implementation of the Golden Rule: "Do unto others as you would have them do unto you."[3]

---

[2] Lk 13:30
[3] Lk 6:31

For Subsidiarity is about *assistance*, not about authority – Subsidiarity illuminates the organization, to make that assistance effective in achieving its purposes. All organizations have some kind of internal structure, which produces order among the components of that organization according to some "layer" or "level" of characteristics of the components. Such organizations also have a fundamental goal or purpose towards which their operations are directed. Subsidiarity simply means that there is a right way of maintaining the relationship between the levels of the organization, in order to accomplish its purpose: specifically, a "higher" level is to support and assist the "lower" levels, but not to interfere with or (as Pius XI said) to arrogate to itself the work of those levels. Subsidiarity produces the "right order" within the organization which is the best way of accomplishing the purpose or design or goal of that organization. Surprisingly, this right order means that the lowest levels are those which most directly achieve the goals, relying on help provided by the higher levels. This order is the inverse of that usually perceived and expected by the modern world, but is both productive as well as just.

As you are about to see, the term "subsidiarity" can also be applied to non-human systems – if only by analogy. This may seem somewhat unusual, but it is nothing more than the device St. Paul used in explaining an even more mystical idea by analogy with the human body:

> For as the body is one and hath many members; and all the
> members of the body, whereas they are many, yet are one body: So
> also is Christ.[4]

This is the beginning of his famous "Analogy of the Body" – indeed, the human body will also play an important role in our discussion.

This scientific, mathematical, and computational approach will help in understanding the design of Subsidiarity, and assist in characterizing its simplicity, its efficiency, and its practicality. All this, we hope, will result in the fuller application of Subsidiarity to all human activities, with a concomitant improvement in the human condition.

---

[4] 1 Cor 12:12

3

Chapter 2
Some History

Paradoxically, Subsidiarity is both new and old. The term, in the sense we use it, dates only to 1963, and even that particular sense was only first sketched in 1891 – but its roots stretch far back into time.

Subsidiarity as an idea is fundamentally a very positive one, arising not from a scheme to *prohibit* but to *assist*. The word itself comes from the Latin military term *subsidium*: originally this meant "the troops stationed in the rear, reserved troops, a reserve, auxiliary forces."[5] Another translation reveals even more: "*subsidium*: the troops stationed in reserve in the third line of battle (behind the *principes*), the line of reserve, reserve-ranks, *triarii*."[6] This definition brings up two important points, which we shall see in greater detail when we explore our example:

(a) This is a *third* line, not a simple main and backup arrangement.

(b) This arrangement specifies the *order of battle*, not of command: that is, this is a *tactical* plan for the purpose of the matters at hand.

To clarify, the order[7] of battle is this:

First line: the *hastati* or spearmen (a *hasta* is a spear or javelin).

Second line: the *principes* (before the *hasta* was introduced, they had been the first-line (the "principal") warriors.

Third line: the *triarii*: the oldest and most experienced Roman soldiers, third behind the other two lines, *ready to help those in need*.

By generalization to non-military use, *subsidium* came to mean a reserve body or an auxiliary corps, and then by abstraction "help, assistance" and "aid, means of aid" and other related meanings. The English words "subsidiary," "subsidy" and "to subsidize" derive from *subsidium*.

I noted that the Latin term refers to the *third* line of defence. It is not merely *another* line, a simply *secondary* line, but the term suggests a more complex structure: a system of *levels* with definite rules governing their interaction, which is what our modern usage implies. This layered idea is much more ancient than Rome. The idea of Subsidiarity, at least in rough form, was suggested to Moses by his father-in-law Jethro. The form may be strikingly familiar to computer scientists:

And the next day Moses sat to judge the people, who stood by Moses from morning until night. And when his kinsman [Jethro] had seen all things that he did among the people, he said: What is it that thou dost among the people? Why sittest thou alone, and all the people wait from morning till night? And Moses answered him:

---

[5] *Cassell's Latin-English and English-Latin Dictionary*, 549
[6] Lewis and Short, *A Latin Dictionary*, 1781
[7] Based on definitions from *Cassell's*.

The people come to me to seek the judgment of God? And when any controversy falleth out among them, they come to me to judge between them, and to shew the precepts of God, and his laws. But he said: The thing thou dost is not good. Thou art spent with foolish labour, both thou, and this people that is with thee; the business is above thy strength, thou alone canst not bear it. But hear my words and counsels, and God shall be with thee. Be thou to the people in those things that pertain to God, to bring their words to him: And to shew the people the ceremonies, and the manner of worshipping; and the way wherein they ought to walk, and the work that they ought to do. And **provide out of all the people able men, such as fear God, in whom there is truth, and that hate avarice, and appoint of them rulers of thousands, and of hundreds, and of fifties, and of tens**, who may judge the people at all times: and **when any great matter soever shall fall out, let them refer it to thee, and let them judge the lesser matters only: that so it may be lighter for thee, the burden being shared out unto others**. If thou dost this, thou shalt fulfil the commandment of God, and shalt be able to bear his precepts: and all this people shall return to their places with peace. And when Moses heard this, he did all things that he had suggested unto him. And choosing able men out of all Israel, he appointed them rulers of the people, rulers over thousands, and over hundreds, and over fifties, and over tens. And they judged the people at all times: and whatsoever was of greater difficulty they referred to him, and they judged the easier cases only. [8]

This raises some interesting questions about the history of Israel, and the subsequent structure of its government. Since there were about 600,000 men (see e.g. Num. 1:46), if the final stage was "rulers of thousands" there would still need to be 600 of these, and so it is not clear whether Jethro's scheme was re-applied so as to reduce the total of those who directly consulted Moses to a reasonable number. While such historical and numerical details need not concern us here, it is certainly stated that Jethro's plan *was* implemented: Moses "did all things that he [Jethro] had suggested"[9] – that is, a layered or "tree-like" arrangement of judges, to simplify the handling of problems among the Israelites, thereby reducing the burden for Moses, and also getting their problems resolved without long waiting periods.

The Greeks and Romans
Plato's *Republic* and Aristotle's *Politics* explore the nature and forms of human organization. Broadly, this was understood according to four levels: the state, the village, the household, the individual. Nature, law, and custom

---

[8] Exodus 18:13-26, emphasis added.
[9] Ex 18:24

established the various necessary relations among these levels. Complications arise in such discussions because these ancient philosophers consistently taught that the State as the highest level of organization was therefore the most important, and the individual (even a citizen) was meaningless in comparison. They also considered slavery as "natural." Such pre-Christian writers lack the understanding of the infinite worth of the human person. Strangely, for all their insistence on the supreme importance of *practicality* – that is, getting the job done – they do not seem to have grasped the higher efficiency which is possible when Subsidiarity is respected.

The Gospels

I might quote just one or two verses of instruction by Jesus, in order to begin suggesting the concept of the levels on which Subsidiarity is built. For example: "He that heareth you heareth Me: and he that despiseth you despiseth Me: and he that despiseth Me despiseth Him that sent Me." "I am the vine; you the branches. He that abideth in Me, and I in him, the same beareth much fruit: for without Me you can do nothing."[10] But there is an episode which will explain the whole thing very nicely:

And the third day, there was a marriage in Cana of Galilee: and the mother of Jesus was there. And Jesus also was invited, and His disciples, to the marriage. And the wine failing, *the mother of Jesus saith to Him: They have no wine.* And Jesus saith to her: Woman, what is that to Me and to thee? My hour is not yet come. *His mother saith to the waiters: Whatsoever he shall say to you, do ye.* Now there were set there six waterpots of stone, according to the manner of the purifying of the Jews, containing two or three measures apiece. Jesus saith to them: Fill the waterpots with water. And they filled them up to the brim. And Jesus saith to them: Draw out now and carry to the chief steward of the feast. And they carried it. And when the chief steward had tasted the water made wine and knew not whence it was, but the waiters knew who had drawn the water: the chief steward calleth the bridegroom, And saith to him: Every man at first setteth forth good wine, and when men have well drunk, then that which is worse. But thou hast kept the good wine until now. [11]

In this very short story, we see Subsidiarity, acting in three levels. The waiters encountered a need they were unable to satisfy. They spoke to Mary regarding that need. She could not satisfy that need herself, so she appealed to her Son. She does not act on, or even interpret His reply, "Woman, what is that..." but simply directs the waiters to carry out whatever He might order. All the deepest aspects and virtues of Subsidiarity are herein exemplified: communication, honesty, humility, trust, obedience. After we have explored

---

[10] Lk 10:16, Jn 15:5
[11] John 2:1-10, emphasis added.

our topic in greater detail, we will again consider the Wedding at Cana in the light of our discoveries.

St. Thomas Aquinas

St. Thomas tells us that it belongs to *wisdom* to set things in order.[12] Thus, our use of wisdom, that greatest of the gifts of the Holy Spirit, must result in *order* in every form of society: family and government, work and recreation, business and education. As we shall see, it is this idea of an ordered society which is the heart of Subsidiarity. And as we might expect, we find important aspects of this topic treated in the most interesting places. For example, in considering God's providence, we read:

> Again. Whoever makes a thing for the sake of an end makes use of it for that end. Now it has been shown above that whatsoever has being in any way is an effect of God: and that God makes all things for an end which is Himself. Therefore He uses everything by directing it to its end. But this is to govern. Therefore God, by His providence, is the Governor of all.[13]

Hiding in the background of our discussions, then, is this fundamental definition: *To govern is to direct things to their end.* That is, the governing or ordering of things has to do with what their "end" or purpose is. We might then expect to find important information when Aquinas deals with the issue of purpose or order. For example, in explaining the existence of chance or luck and its relation to God, we find this important detail:

> ...the diversity of order in causes must be in keeping with diversity of order among things. ... It belongs to the order of divine providence that there be order and degrees among causes. The higher a cause is above its effect, the greater its power, so that its causality extends to a greater number of things. But the intention of a natural cause never extends further than its power: for such an intention would be in vain. Consequently the intention of an individual cause cannot possibly extend to all possible contingencies.[14]

And in the consideration of the existence of evil, which is a purpose contrary to God's purpose, there is this:

> In every government the best thing is that provision be made for the things governed, according to their mode: for in this consists the justice of the regime. Consequently even as it would be contrary to the right notion of human rule, if the governor of a state were to forbid men to act according to their various duties – except perhaps for the time being, on account of some particular urgency.... ... The good of the whole is of more account than the good of the part. Therefore it belongs to a prudent governor to overlook a lack of

[12] Aquinas, *Summa Theologica* II-II Q45 A6, quoting Aristotle's *Metaphysics* I:2
[13] Aquinas, *Summa Contra Gentiles* Book 3 Chapter 64
[14] Aquinas, *Summa Contra Gentiles* Book 3 Chapter 74

goodness in a part, that there may be an increase of goodness in the whole: thus the builder hides the foundation of a house underground, that the whole house may stand firm.[15]

Speaking of order, it is no pun that the name of the sacrament of the priesthood is Holy Orders. Aquinas explains the nature of order in general, in preparation for a discussion of that sacrament:

A power directed to a principal effect naturally has lesser powers administering to it. This may be clearly seen in the arts: the arts which dispose the material are subservient to the art which introduces the art-form: and the art that introduces the art-form is subservient to the art which is concerned with the end of the art-product: and again the art that is concerned with an anterior end is subservient to the art that is concerned with the ultimate end. Thus the art of wood-cutting serves the ship-building art; and the latter serves the art of sailing; and this latter serves the art of commerce or war or the like, in so far as sailing may be directed to various ends.[16]

While the above excerpts assist us in the broad view of government and organization, we have not yet touched on the sense of interrelation between these orders which is the deeper character of Subsidiarity. As above, we find choice hints in the most curious places: for example, in considering the question "Whether it is lawful for the accused to escape judgment by appealing?" Aquinas rebuts an argument in these words:

A man should submit to the lower authority in so far as the latter observes the order of the higher authority. If the lower authority departs from the order of the higher, we ought not to submit to it, for instance "if the proconsul order one thing and the emperor another," according to a gloss on Rm. 13:2. Now when a judge oppresses anyone unjustly, in this respect he departs from the order of the higher authority, whereby he is obliged to judge justly. Hence it is lawful for a man who is oppressed unjustly, to have recourse to the authority of the higher power, by appealing either before or after sentence has been pronounced. [17]

And as Aquinas begins to study the concept of the failure of order called "sin," he explains the ordering of all human behavior:

...there should be a threefold order in man: one in relation to the rule of reason, in so far as all our actions and passions should be commensurate with the rule of reason: another order is in relation to the rule of the Divine Law, whereby man should be directed in all things: and if man were by nature a solitary animal, this twofold order would suffice. But since man is naturally a civic and social animal, as is proved in [Aristotle's] *Politics* i, 2, hence a third order

---

[15] Aquinas, *Summa Contra Gentiles* Book 3 Chapter 71
[16] Aquinas, *Summa Contra Gentiles* Book 4 Chapter 75
[17] Aquinas, *Summa Theologica* II-II Q69 A3 *ad* 1

is necessary, whereby man is directed in relation to other men among whom he has to dwell.[18]

As we shall see, Subsidiarity acts according to this threefold order:

(1) According to the rule of reason, as means are directed to an end, because Subsidiarity is about the accomplishment of a purpose.

(2) According to the rule of Divine Law, by which we know we are not our own ends. Our ultimate purpose is in God, and all lesser purposes must tend towards that purpose, so (consistent with the Great Command, Dt 6:4-5), we must use all our power in the performance of God's will: so Subsidiarity means that we must both provide assistance when called upon, and seek aid when we need it.

(3) According to the direction in relation to other men, because from the beginning God said "it is not good for Man to be alone"[19] and that society is to be governed by the "Golden Rule."[20]

Thus, Subsidiarity means that we must be as ready to assist others as we would want them to be ready to provide us with assistance.

Cardinal Newman's *The Idea of a University*

One of the most important tasks of a computer programmer is debugging: that is, studying a problem, defect, or failure in order to find out what went wrong – then formulating a correction to keep the problem from recurring. Other fields have similar tasks: Aquinas does not simply state a truth or merely propose an argument: he gives the objections of others, *and then replies to them*. More recently, John Henry Cardinal Newman did something similar in his 1852 exploration of higher education called *The Idea of a University*. Chief among the defects he noted was the failure of universities to be *universal*: they omitted or belittled one or another field of study, with the result that its proper subject was then absorbed or appropriated by other fields. (Newman applied this argument to Theology as a special case, but 150 years later the same error is still being made, with respect to theology and to other fields.) Newman's discussion applies to our topic because it reveals the importance of the *fundamental purpose of the system* – when that purpose is violated, the system fails.

Newman studied that vast and complex human system which is the transmission of knowledge: a University is about knowledge, and knowledge is about truth, and truth requires the activity of all the fields of study. Hence, he pointed out, the omission of one component destroys the equilibrium of the whole system of knowledge:

> To blot it out is nothing short, if I may so speak, of unravelling the web of University Teaching. ... if you drop any science out of the circle of knowledge, you cannot keep its place vacant for it; that science is forgotten; the other sciences close up, or, in other words,

---

[18] Ibid., I-II Q72 A4
[19] Gn 2:18
[20] Lk 6:31

they exceed their proper bounds, and intrude where they have no right. ... a science which exceeds its limits falls into error. [21]

As we shall see, this sounds very much like a failure in Subsidiarity. Newman proceeds to set forth even more important points which we shall see in greater detail:

The human mind cannot keep from speculating and systematizing; and if Theology is not allowed to occupy its own territory, adjacent sciences, nay, sciences which are quite foreign to Theology, will take possession of it. And this occupation is proved to be a usurpation by this circumstance, that these foreign sciences will assume certain principles as true, and act upon them, which *they neither have authority to lay down themselves, nor appeal to any other higher science to lay down for them.* [22]

Observe carefully the structure Newman is sketching out: a *system of sciences* – that is, of *all* fields of study, not only the technical ones – all working in pursuit of knowledge and of truth, but each in its own specialized manner, and according to its own proper rules.

Newman's work, then, provides several ideas which are important to our topic: the idea of a system which has been set up for some purpose; the idea of a system which is dependent upon the proper *and united* functioning of every one of its components if its purpose is to be attained; the idea that the components are specialized in their various tasks, in pursuit of the fundamental purpose of the system. Also, he warns of the system's failure arising from unjust intrusion of one domain into another, and suggests that within the system there could be higher levels of authority to which appeal can be made when special cases must be addressed. Thus we begin to see hints of the great things which came not quite forty years later.

---

[21] Newman, *The Idea of a University* 64, 67; emphasis added.
[22] Ibid., 87-88; emphasis added.

Chapter 3
The Modern Era: "Catholic Social Teaching"

Rerum Novarum

The idea of Subsidiarity was first sketched by Leo XIII in his famous encyclical, *Rerum Novarum*, published in 1891. He founded the idea upon the family, setting it in logical opposition to the State – and thereby inverting the hierarchy which puts the State ahead of its components. Chesterton uses this inverted, upside-down view to indicate the correct perception of reality:

> ...you remember that he [Peter] was crucified upside down. I've often fancied his humility was rewarded by seeing in death the beautiful vision of his boyhood. He also saw the landscape as it really is: with the stars like flowers, and the clouds like hills, and all men hanging on the mercy of God. [23]

Indeed, Leo XIII's work seems dramatically linked to Chesterton's, in showing the importance of distinguishing things which need to be kept separate. Consider that Jesus said "Think ye, that I am come to give peace on earth? I tell you, no; but separation"[24] and Chesterton's insightful inversion of Mt 19:6: "Those whom God has sundered, shall no man join."[25] In the same manner, Leo XIII divided the social *system* into State and Family.

Having effected the correct separation of the components in the social system, Leo then restored order to it by lifting up the lowest part. This lesson, as Chesterton pointed out, "is the lesson of 'Cinderella' which is the same as that of the Magnificat – *exaltavit humiles*."[26] Henceforth as Jesus predicted, the lowest was to rank ahead of the highest: "And behold, they are last that shall be first: and they are first that shall be last."[27] And we shall see this in even greater detail, because "That is the paradox of the whole position; that henceforth the highest thing can only work from below."[28]

Here, then, is the kernel element, or necessary foundation, of Subsidiarity: The system is composed of parts, and the parts form a *hierarchy* – an ordered arrangement of layers – within the system. With this in mind, let us see how Leo proceeds:

> 20. It is a most sacred law of nature that the father of a family see that his offspring are provided with all the necessities of life, and nature even prompts him to desire to provide and to furnish his children, who, in fact reflect and in a sense continue his person, with the means of decently protecting themselves against harsh fortune in the uncertainties of life. He can do this surely in no other way than by owning fruitful goods to transmit by inheritance to his

---

[23] GKC *The Poet and the Lunatics* 21-22
[24] Lk 12:51
[25] GKC, *The Common Man* 143
[26] GKC, *Orthodoxy* CW1:253, quoting Lk 1:52 (Vulgate); the Latin means "He has lifted up the lowly."
[27] Lk 13:30
[28] GKC, *The Everlasting Man* CW2:313. Also cf. Jn 13:2-15

children. As already noted, the family like the State is by the same token a society in the strictest sense of the term, and is governed by its own proper authority, namely, by that of the father. Wherefore, assuming, of course, that those limits be observed which are fixed by its immediate purpose, the family assuredly possesses rights, at least equal with those of civil society, in respect to choosing and employing the things necessary for its protection and its just liberty. We say "at least equal" because, inasmuch as domestic living together is prior both in thought and in fact to uniting into a polity, it follows that its rights and duties are also prior and more in conformity with nature. But if citizens, if families, after becoming participants in common life and society, were to experience injury in a commonwealth instead of help, impairment of their rights instead of protection, society would be something to be repudiated rather than to be sought for.

21. To desire, therefore, that the civil power should enter arbitrarily into the privacy of homes is a great and pernicious error. If a family perchance is in such extreme difficulty and is so completely without plans that it is entirely unable to help itself, it is right that the distress be remedied by public aid, for each individual family is a part of the community. Similarly, if anywhere there is a grave violation of mutual rights within the family walls, public authority shall restore to each his right; for this is not usurping the rights of citizens, but protecting and confirming them with just and due care. Those in charge of public affairs, however, must stop here; nature does not permit them to go beyond these limits. Paternal authority is such that it can be neither abolished nor absorbed by the State, because it has the same origin in common with that of man's own life. "Children are a part of their father," and, as it were, a kind of extension of the father's person; and, strictly speaking, not through themselves, but through the medium of the family society in which they are begotten, they enter into and participate in civil society. And for the very reason that children "are by nature part of their father...before they have the use of free will, they are kept under the care of their parents." [Aquinas, *Summa Theologica*, II-II Q10A12] Inasmuch as the Socialists, therefore, disregard care by parents and in its place introduce care by the State, they act against natural justice and dissolve the structure of the home.[29]

From this excerpt, Leo XIII might be said to be the "founder" of Subsidiarity – but he did *not* use that word in *Rerum Novarum*.

I wish I had room to explore the extent to which this great document influenced Chesterton. It may be the substrate on which he built his *What's Wrong With the World* (1910) and *The Outline of Sanity* (1926), and he seems to have made occasional indirect reference to it,[30] but it was so much

---

[29] *Rerum Novarum* (1891)

in his mind that in 1926 he mentioned it in a mystery story.[31] Also, he seems to allude to the final sentence of paragraph 20 ("But if citizens...") in his *The Ball and the Cross* where he writes: "If the citizen finds himself despoiled of such pleasures and powers as he would have had even in the savage state, the social contract is annulled."[32]

Forty Years Later

But in the Roman Catholic Church, *Rerum Novarum* had a very significant effect. So important did this encyclical prove – the first of the "modern" studies of Church teaching on human society – that in 1931 Pope Pius XI wrote an encyclical, *Quadragesimo Anno*, specifically commemorating its fortieth anniversary.

It is indeed true, as history clearly proves, that owing to the change in social conditions, much that was formerly done by small bodies can nowadays be accomplished only by large corporations. None the less, just as it is wrong to withdraw from the individual and commit to the community at large what private enterprise and industry can accomplish, so, too, *it is an injustice, a grave evil and a disturbance of right order for a larger and higher organization to arrogate to itself functions which can be performed efficiently by smaller and lower bodies*. This is a fundamental principle of social philosophy, unshaken and unchangeable... [33]

Here, Pius gives a succinct and general (though negative) form of the concept – yet we still do not have the term "subsidiarity." It is this encyclical, however, not Leo's, which most later documents give as a reference.

John XXIII Gives Us the Term

John XXIII released his *Mater Et Magistra* in 1961, seventy years after Leo XIII's work, examining the topic in ever greater detail, and with ever greater concern. Here, the idea proposed by Leo and discussed by Pius is finally given a distinguishing name.

52. But – for reasons explained by Our predecessors – the civil power must also have a hand in the economy. It has to promote production in a way best calculated to achieve social progress and the well-being of all citizens.

53. And in this work of directing, stimulating, co-ordinating, supplying and integrating, its guiding principle must be the "principle of subsidiary function" formulated by Pius XI in *Quadragesimo Anno*, "This is a fundamental principle of social philosophy, unshaken and unchangeable... Just as it is wrong to withdraw from the individual and commit to a community what

---

[30] E.g., ILN essay for Nov. 17, 1923 CW33:216-217; *The Everlasting Man* CW2:186; *St. Thomas Aquinas* CW2:544

[31] GKC, "The Oracle of the Dog" in *The Incredulity of Father Brown*, CW13:83.

[32] GKC, *The Ball and the Cross*, CW7:251.

[33] *Quadragesimo Anno* (1931) emphasis added

private enterprise and industry can accomplish, so too it is an injustice, a grave evil and a disturbance of right order, for a larger and higher association to arrogate to itself functions which can be performed efficiently by smaller and lower societies. Of its very nature the true aim of all social activity should be to help members of the social body, but never to destroy or absorb them."

54. The present advance in scientific knowledge and productive technology clearly puts it within the power of the public authority to a much greater degree than ever before to reduce imbalances which may exist between different branches of the economy or between different regions within the same country or even between the different peoples of the world. It also puts into the hands of public authority a greater means for limiting fluctuations in the economy and for providing effective measures to prevent the recurrence of mass unemployment. Hence the insistent demands on those in authority – since they are responsible for the common good – to increase the degree and scope of their activities in the economic sphere, and to devise ways and means and set the necessary machinery in motion for the attainment of this end.

55. But however extensive and far-reaching the influence of the State on the economy may be, it must never be exerted to the extent of depriving the individual citizen of his freedom of action. It must rather augment his freedom while effectively guaranteeing the protection of his essential personal rights. Among these is a man's right and duty to be primarily responsible for his own upkeep and that of his family. Hence every economic system must permit and facilitate the free development of productive activity.[34]

Just two years later, the cumbersome "the principle of subsidiary function" was reduced to the simpler term "subsidiarity" – which appeared for the first time in John XXIII's *Pacem in Terris*, as he applied it to a system even larger than the Family/State of Leo:

140. Moreover, just as it is necessary in each state that relations which the public authority has with its citizens, families and intermediate associations be controlled and regulated by *the principle of subsidiarity*, it is equally necessary that the relationships which exist between the world-wide public authority and the public authority of individual nations be governed by the same principle. This means that the world-wide public authority must tackle and solve problems of an economic, social, political or cultural character which are posed by the universal common good. For, because of the vastness, complexity and urgency of those problems, the public authorities of the individual states are not in a position to tackle them with any hope of a positive solution. [35]

---

[34] *Mater et Magistra* (1961)
[35] *Pacem in Terris* (1963) emphasis added

The idea, though not the term, was evident in Paul VI's Apostolic Letter *Octogesima Adveniens* in 1971, commemorating the 80th anniversary of Leo's work. Similarly, the 90th anniversary was commemorated by John Paul II's *Laborem Exercens*, dealing with the nature of human work.

One hundred years after Leo's work, sixty after Pius XI's "negative" form, and nearly forty after John XIII's first use of the term, John Paul II gives this "positive" definition of Subsidiarity in the work specifically celebrating the centennial of *Rerum Novarum*:

48. Here again the principle of subsidiarity must be respected: a community of a higher order should not interfere in the internal life of a community of a lower order, depriving the latter of its functions, but rather should support it in case of need and help to coordinate its activity with the activities of the rest of society, always with a view to the common good.[36]

Just nine years later, the above passage was put into the source code for a computer program, and a high-tech company came to rely on Subsidiarity.

I will now proceed to tell you about it.

---

[36] *Centesimus Annus* (1991)

Part II
An Example of Subsidiarity: Ad Insertion for Cable TV

"I am the vine: you the branches. He that abideth in Me, and I in him,
the same beareth much fruit: for without Me you can do nothing." Jn 15:5

How can I understand, unless some man show me? Acts 8:31

Chapter 1
Why use cable TV as an example?

Why am I going to explain Subsidiarity with such a strange thing as cable television? Well, the whole point of this book is to explain *subsidiarity*. But as soon as I mention this word, I will get objections like these:

"**Subsidiarity is abstract.**" They mean it is just an idea, and is applicable only to ideas.

"**Subsidiarity is theoretical.**" They mean it's abstract, or that it is at most a proposal, and not practical in the *real* world.

"**Subsidiarity is 'religious'.**" That "religious" term usually means "Catholic" – and that means it will involve "worship" or "dogma" or something spiritual, possibly the Pope, or other elements of Catholicism.

"**Subsidiarity is too hard to do anything with.**" This is usually just a way of intensifying the "abstract" or "theoretical" objections.

"**Subsidiarity is technical.**" And besides, it will involve hard words like "hierarchy" which suggests that "religious" thing again.

"**Subsidiarity is complicated.**" Another intensifier of negativity like "too hard" or "technical"; see above.

"**Subsidiarity is unpractical.**" This is obviously related to the first two, or perhaps three points, as the other terms never bother people in fields like the automotive industry, aviation, electronics, and so on.

My reply? Maybe it was once. *But not any more!* I defeat *all* the objections with one counterexample, as we do in mathematics. Moreover, I did not pick this example. It was quite the other way around.

Though once you have read the rest of this book, I am not sure that you will agree that I have defeated the "too hard" or "too complicated" objections. All I can say is that you must apply those terms to my explanation, or my example, and not to *subsidiarity* – because it really is almost too simple to explain. Or, as GKC would say, it's too big to be seen.

Perhaps it is well that there are a number of hard and complex points to my example, for these have helped bring out more subtleties than a simple example would. And no merely technical system, no matter how much specialized jargon and intricate mathematics it may require, can ever be as complex as any human organization.

However, whatever else you learn from my explanation, I hope you will understand this: my example is not a contrived one, just a dream in my brain or a sketch on paper. It was a real company with a real, functioning system, delivering some 200,000 spots which played over 200 million times during the five and a half years it was running. (I'd love to quote the dollar amount involved but I never learned what it was.) And leaving intangibles such as prayer (e.g. "Oh God, I hope it works this time.") for discussion elsewhere, I can also assert that there was nothing specifically Catholic about the machinery or the software, except, of course, that this "subsidiarity" term first appeared in an encyclical. (We can ignore incidentals like quoting *Centesimus Annus* in the source code.)

Hence it is reasonable to say that this example was definitely not abstract, not theory, not tied to any religion, and very certainly practical. Our major customer (a nationally known cable company) certainly thought so, or they wouldn't have paid our bills.

A different preliminary apology – or explanation

Perhaps you are finding the title of this part of the book something of a surprise. I can understand that. We were all surprised, in the company where I used to work, back in late 1999, when we were puzzling over how we were going to handle certain activities in the ad insertion system we were implementing. But whether one merely calls it an analogy, or one writes a technical paper trying to describe it, or one ignores it, the system *worked*, and many of my co-workers came to know the term "subsidiarity" for that part of the system.

Nice, isn't it?

Yes, well, you would like to hear more. And that is my problem. I am having a very difficult time writing this part, because I want to tell you the exciting part, but there is so much to tell so that you will understand that it really is exciting. And there is the related difficulty: why should I explain *an example* – and a *complex example* at that – when perhaps I should be explaining Subsidiarity? That's my whole point.

Perhaps if I were a philosopher, or some other kind of scholar, I could do that. I have given you a taste of the historical view already. But I have to face it: I am a computer scientist, and a Chestertonian at that, so the way in which I explain something is going to come out that way, flavoured, if I may so put it, with beer and binary. And just in case you are worried that I am going to give you a lot of very technical details – no, I won't do that. I want to give you just enough of the problem and the project, and the way our system worked, so that we can talk about that system, and learn from it. It will make the big topic much easier, for I will be talking about *real, accomplished events*: not about a hope, or a plan, or an abstraction, or a wish – and it is this real experience, just like any scientific experiment, which has the power to communicate the far more difficult (and philosophical) details, which is my purpose.

What I am NOT going to tell you...

I *am* going to tell you a number of things about a rather technical system – the hidden world of cable TV advertising. Some of them are still true, but some others have long since gone into the past with eight-tracks, buggy whips and oil lamps. But this is *not* a book about cable TV, nor about ad insertion – it's not a "how-to" book in that fashion. Nor am I going to justify *why* we decided to do certain things, or argue about alternatives. The topic will be detailed enough to manage without going down all the many dead-ends in the thorny maze of system design that we once struggled through. I also omit a large number of dull technical matters which are necessary to actually build such a system.

Restricted to an Analogy

Father Stanley L. Jaki is the author of over forty books dealing with the details of the history of science and the relation between science and religion. We met at a Chesterton Conference and I mentioned my work on ad insertion, saying that I had "implemented Subsidiarity in software." He pointed out that "subsidiarity" was properly applied to human organizations, indicating that it was not correct to apply it to a mechanical or non-human construction. As I am neither a philosopher nor a theologian, I made no attempt to debate the matter – and therefore I proposed that if I ever wrote about Subsidiarity, I would portray my work as an "analogy" or "example" proposed for the sake of discussion. I have not been quite so rigid in my usage in this book, but I want to be clear on this: I have not done so because I disagree with him. I merely plead habit. I have gotten used to thinking of Subsidiarity as applying to wider schemes. But he is right, and I will try to explain why.

In fact, one learns quite a lot from the restriction. As usual when discussing humans, we see a paradox: the restriction narrows even as it broadens the discussion. For there is a fundamental issue at stake in the human sphere, and a much debated one – it is called *free will*. A computer or machine or system of machines cannot choose to act against its nature, its design or its instructions – when it does, we say "it failed" or "it has a bug" – and then we repair or replace it, or we design and build a better one.

But humans can lie and distort, they can be lazy, or traitorous, or inattentive, or stupid, or selfish. But they can also be dependable – extraordinarily so, in fact, as you will learn from this example. They can be honest, generous, outgoing, responsive, innovative, and self-sacrificing. So the picture is indeed far more complex when limited to humans alone, and yet the Jaki restriction points out certain aspects of Subsidiarity which need to be addressed. I am not going to go into any moral aspects here, though the discussion definitely belongs to that branch of philosophy.

OK (whew) all the introductory warnings are out of the way. So then let us begin, with the help ✠ of God, Who made heaven and earth...

Chapter 2
Things You Need To Know

This chapter introduces some basic ideas about cable TV, ad insertion, and our company. In the next chapter you'll see them at work.

What We're Trying To Do

Here's what we do – well, what we *did* at the company where I used to work, but it gets tedious putting it in the past, so for best results, just imagine it is late 2000.

Just as national businesses advertise on cable TV, so do local businesses. But a local company like a restaurant is not likely to want costly advertising on a national scale. The early part of the procedure is the same for both: they arrange to have commercials made which give information about their products and services.. These commercials are usually produced as 30 second long "clips" – chunks of video and audio – kept on a video tape similar to those you play on your VCR, but of higher quality. The difference comes in how a *local* commercial is gotten into the cable TV system.

Our company receives these tapes, as well as specifications about where and when that commercial should be played – that is, the dates and times and desired repetitions, as well as the TV networks and the geographical regions – the *when* and the *where* – in which the commercials are to be played. We take those tapes (we call them spots for short), process them so we can play them, and build all the machinery so that they can be played (or *inserted*) into the cable TV distribution system. We set up schedules for playing, send out the spots to the places where they get played according to those schedules, and monitor all that machinery as it performs its work. Finally, since we're providing a service for these businesses, we'll charge them for playing their spots, so we'll have to keep some kind of record of each performance.

The commercial on tape is encoded and it becomes a file

We are given the spot on a tape, but we're going to play it on a computerized device. So the spot must be *encoded*. We have a special piece of equipment called the *encoder* which transforms the audio and video into a digital form. The audio and video of that spot is now contained in a file, and so it can be stored in a computer and played back. Also, since it is a file, it can be transported over a computer network. Remember, when a computer copies a file, the result is *identical* to the original, just in a different location – and the original is unchanged.

Cable TV is distributed to you (the viewer) from headends

You may be surprised to learn that the wire connected to your TV does *not* go all the way to the studios of the various TV networks you receive. Its source is in a local "substation" called a *headend*, often located on a nearby hilltop. The headend is a small building full of equipment, surrounded by a number of satellite dishes and other antennas, which acquire the signals from the various TV network studios. The headend equipment receives, transforms, and unites these signals, then sends them out (through the cable) to the viewers.

Some important things to know about the headends:
1. Most headends are out in the middle of nowhere, and at that time (late 2000) were not able to be connected to the INTERNET.

2. The available open space in a typical headend is very limited.

3. Any given headend may handle 24 or more TV networks.

4. Inside the headend, each TV network is *separate* from other TV networks, until the point where they are all put together before being sent out to the viewers.

5. All of the headends together are called *the Field*.

The inserter – the machine at the headend that plays spots
We built a special kind of computer called an *inserter* which can play the digital form of a spot using a "playback device." Our inserters contained up to eight of these playback devices. As you may be aware, computers are limited in space: sooner or later, there's no room to add any more devices inside the box. Also, even though we used very large disk drives (the place where the computer stores its files), providing us with far more disk space than typical home computers of that day, there is still only so much space available. But the inserter can take care of things like when to play a spot, and which TV network it should be played on, and keeping track of what it has played.

The inserter is important to our discussion, so I want you to have a good mental picture of it. Picture a big black box, about a foot high and two feet wide, and maybe three feet long. It weighs about 80 pounds. There is a power cord, and eight *inbound* pairs of cables and eight *outbound* pairs of cables. There are eight for each of the eight TV networks this inserter can handle: each pair carries the audio and the video signals. Normally those signals from each TV network flow into the inbound side, through the inserter, and out the outbound side. But when the time is right, the inserter breaks that flow, and *inserts* (plays back) the required spot according to its instructions.

There is also a computer network cable which links together all of the inserters at that headend – but it is only a local computer network, and only those few machines in that headend are linked together by it.

Finally, at each headend there is one small satellite dish which is connected to one special inserter. That inserter is called the *portal*. The portal is able to communicate over a satellite connection with the Headquarters of our company, which I must now tell you about.

Our Headquarters (the human part)
Our corporate office has all the usual components of any other company. It also has a number of special departments which handle the various aspects of our task. You will hear more about them as we proceed. Briefly, they are

the people who talk with our customers, do scheduling and billing, encode the spots and monitor the equipment, take care of our headend machinery, and build, test, and repair the equipment. They are organized into these departments:

Ad Sales – if you want a spot played, this is where you go. Our customers, who are marketing reps from various companies, have their Sales Representative here – they receive the tapes and instructions on how the spots are to be played.

Traffic – they receive the tapes and instructions from Ad Sales, and perform the scheduling of the spot plays, as well as billing. They use special software (the "Traffic and Billing system") to accomplish these tasks.

Operations – this 24/7 department is always open, keeping watch over the machinery by the various monitors in the Control Room. They also convert tapes to a digital form using special tools called *encoders*.

Field Services – they install, repair, and replace equipment at the headends in the Field.

Tech Shop – they build and repair inserters and other equipment.

Our Headquarters (the machine part)

There are a number of computers and other equipment at our corporate site. Briefly, these machines do the scheduling and billing, encoding and storage of spots, transport from and to the Field, and the monitoring of both these machines and those in the Field. Most of this equipment is kept in a special air-conditioned computer room; the Control Room contains the encoders and monitoring equipment. Here are the major components involved in our example:

The Big Dish – the first thing people notice when they came to visit was the big satellite transmitting dish out in back, which is the visible part of the satellite transport machinery. Inside our building are the transmitters, receivers, and other electronic equipment.

HOME – connected to the satellite machinery is the main computer in charge of transport, which we call *HOME*. (There's no place like it.) This computer performs the actual transport of files to the Field.

MASTER LIBRARY – a large storage area where the spots are kept; it is connected to HOME, and is really nothing more than a very large disk drive. (It was bought in 1999 and at that time, 3 terabytes, or 3 trillion characters, was a *large* amount of storage.)

Encoders – these are special computers, connected to the MASTER LIBRARY, and linked to video-tape players (VTRs) and various pieces of measuring equipment. The Operations department uses them to transform the commercials on the tapes into an electronic form, which is checked for proper quality by the measuring equipment.

Monitors – there are a number of monitoring computers connected with the other machinery; their displays keep the Operations department informed about the status of the machinery both locally (which we call the Home Cluster) and remotely (the Field).

The **_Traffic and Billing_ system** – these computers are used by Traffic to perform scheduling (also known as "traffic") and billing.

Chapter 3
Spot Transport for Local Ad Insertion

Let's say it is late 2000. You have a television in your house. You have cable. You and the gang are watching a show, and just at the exciting part, there's a commercial break: Hey, there's "Joe's Bait and Tackle Shop" down on Route 30. And Vince's, remember, where they have those great wings? – hey, guys, they have all-you-can-eat this Wednesday! *Another* used-car ad – gimme a break! Ah, finally: back to the show...

Television commercials for companies in your local area are called *local spots*. The owner, or perhaps the marketing department of the business decided on getting a 30-second commercial put together. So a script was written, a production house went there with cameras, and after some video editing, they were handed a cassette – more-or-less like the ones you use in your home VCR, but usually of a higher quality.

But, you may wonder, what is Marta, the owner at Vince's, going to do with that cassette containing the spot she paid for? Where is she going to play it so that you will see it at your home, and hopefully come and eat wings next Wednesday?

Well, let's trace the cable from the back of your set, and see where it goes.... Out of the house, through some equipment on a nearby utility pole, through cable over some miles... ah, what's this? High atop a hill, down the road from your house, there is a low bunker-like building, almost hidden in the trees. Over on the hillside are a number of satellite dishes, and tall red and white antennas high in the air. That building is packed with electronic equipment for handling the various networks which are supplied to the customers on that local part of the cable system. This whole installation is called the *headend* for that area. Inside the headend, our cable goes through various kinds of equipment – and suddenly we find that the signal for that network comes in from one of those dishes out on the hillside. That signal comes from the *national feed* of that network, sent out to the entire nation from that network's central location.

You shrug to yourself. If that signal is *national*, there's no way that it could contain the commercial for a *local* business. (Unless, of course, your "local" business serves the whole country – but we're talking about truly local businesses.) How about all that equipment in the headend, then? Yes, this is where each of the various TV networks are received, each from its own dish or antenna, and through its own specially tuned equipment, and just before those networks are brought together so they can be sent out (over the cable) to the viewing public – yes, here is the place where these local spots can be *inserted*. We use that term because the spot is *inserted* into the normal stream of programming coming from a particular TV network. The national feed is always showing *something* during a commercial break – but at certain times the networks will permit the insertion of local spots.

So that means we're going to need some equipment – something like a VCR to play our tape, and we're going to need to know *when* we're allowed to play that spot. (Otherwise we'll interrupt the normal programming of the network, and that will make the viewers very upset.) But, as you look around the headend, you see that there's no one here. (You and I have special permission to visit today, sort of like the Ghost of Christmas Present.) It's not a very comfortable place, as you can see, and there's hardly room to move around. And after all, no one is going to want to sit in this room full of equipment waiting just to press a button to play a commercial. So we're going to have to use some more equipment to do the ad insertion. And with all this equipment already here, we're going to be limited as to how much more we can add. (Fortunately, we do not have to use VCRs in the headends any more.)

The Inserter

The piece of equipment we use to do local ad insertion is called an *inserter*. It is really just a computer with special "playback" devices, one for each network it is to do insertion for. The inserter has to have storage for all the spots it is going to play, and other things like a clock so it knows when to play them, and some arrangement for instructions (we call this a *schedule*) about what spot it is to play at what time. One other thing is required: it must keep a record (we call this a *spot-log*) of what it has done, so that the local businesses can be billed once their spots have been played.

The inserter is therefore just a kind of automated "spot jukebox" which plays different commercials on the various networks and remembers what it did for billing purposes. OK, but we are out here in this headend on a hillside, and so we must consider how the schedules and spots get to the inserter, and the spot-logs come back. But first I must mention two characteristics of the inserter which are critical to our topic.

1. This particular inserter can only handle up to *eight* TV networks at once. (There's only so much room inside these computers, after all.) But the cable company wants to be able to show local spots on 24 or more networks – so that means we shall need three or more inserters to handle the work in a headend.

2. The spots will be stored on the disk drive inside the computer – a *large* disk drive – but even a very large disk can get full. So we can only keep a limited number of spots in any given inserter. Also, for technical reasons, whatever spot we wish to play *has to be on the disk of the inserter playing it*. Even though the three or more inserters will be connected together on a small computer network, the spots always have to be locally present. And in case you're thinking that this small network is connected to other computers – sorry. It isn't like that. In the days we're discussing, the INTERNET did *not* reach to all these headends, and even for those it did reach, other limitations came into effect. So we had to use a different technique.

Communication with the Headend

For a number of technical reasons which are not relevant to our discussion, we used a special form of satellite communication called *VSAT* to communicate between our Headquarters and the headends. There was a large "outbound" channel, so we could send the spots to the headends, but only a small "inbound" channel, which was enough to handle bringing back the spot-logs, and other status information. We had a big satellite transmitting dish out in back of our Headquarters, and each headend had one single small transmitting dish. (There was no room for more than one.) The inserter which had the dish was called the *portal* because it was the "door" or "gateway" to the rest of our world. The other inserters were called *leaves* because they sprouted off from the portal – and the whole collection of inserters at a headend was called a *subtree*.

And now, stop for a moment and think – can you see what's coming? Remember: (1) an inserter can handle no more than 8 networks; (2) at a typical headend, we will need to perform ad insertion on 24 or more networks; thus a headend will require *three or more inserters*. But we were permitted to install *only one* small satellite dish at the headend, and that dish can connect to only one inserter. Thus, the combination of these limitations proved to be the "necessity" which mothered the "invention" of what we came to call Subsidiarity in our system.

Our Headquarters

As I have mentioned, there was the big dish out in back of our Headquarters. Connected to the satellite communications equipment was a computer called *HOME* which was in charge of the Headquarters side of transport. Connected to HOME was the MASTER LIBRARY which contained all the spots presently in use. There were devices called *encoders* which performed the conversion of the spots from the tape form into the digital form called MPEG; the spot was then put into the MASTER LIBRARY. Other computers provided a means of monitoring what was going on throughout the system. Finally, there was another computer system called *Traffic and Billing* which produced the schedules and processed the spot-logs, and finally billed the customers.

The Tech Shop

First, the inserters must be built by the technicians in the Tech Shop. That means the various special components, such as the eight playback devices, must be mounted inside the computer; then all the programs are loaded and everything is set up so that it is ready to do its work. Then the inserter is tested with a dummy "test schedule" and after it has performed correctly, it is ready for use in the Field.

Field Services

This department is the most mobile of the parts of the company: they are the ones who perform the installation (the original set-up) of the inserters and other equipment (like the small dish) in headends anywhere throughout the Field (an area over 100 miles in radius). If an inserter fails to perform correctly, the Field Tech drives there with tools and equipment, usually including a spare inserter, investigates the problem, and does whatever is necessary to correct it. This department has someone on-call, ready to respond at any time of the day or night.

Ad Sales

When Marta from Vince's Restaurant wants to have her spot played, she will talk to her customer representative in the Ad Sales department. He will let her know what networks are available, and in what localities her spots can be seen. Once he knows the networks she wants her spot to play on, he can see what times and dates are available. He accumulates all this information and produces an "order" for the play of the spot on particular networks, at particular headends, at given dates and times.

Traffic

The order and the tape then come to the Traffic department, where a Traffic Coordinator will assign an identifying number or code (we call it the *spot id*) to the spot on the tape, writing it on a "traffic slip." This spot id, together with the other information on the order from Ad Sales, will be put into the Traffic and Billing machinery, which will produce a schedule which is then sent to the relevant headends.

Operations

The tape, with its attached "traffic slip" indicating the id for the spot, is taken to the Operations department. There, an operator will perform the encoding procedure, which converts the spot into its digital form (which is just a big computer file), and assigns the specified spot id to that file. The digital spot is checked for correctness, then it goes into the MASTER LIBRARY.

Where Subsidiarity Comes In

At this point, the spot in its digital form is stored in the MASTER LIBRARY, which is connected to HOME, the computer which handles spot transport. Remember that the inserters out at the various headends are the machines which actually play the spots. Any given inserter can play the spots it has on its own disk drive. But if the spot to be played is not present, there must be some way of getting the spot to the places which need it. Most inserters are *leaves* within a given headend, which means they can communicate only with their portal. The portal is the only means of communication with HOME, which is the machine at Headquarters that handles spot transport to the portals. HOME has access to the spots stored in the MASTER LIBRARY, and it can inform Operations of its current status by means of the various monitoring equipment.

It is this three-layered structure (leaf, portal, HOME) which suggested the idea of Subsidiarity back in late 1999. The method relies on a simple idea: someone who needs a spot "appeals" to one who is able to *help* – that is, able to satisfy that need.

We shall now proceed through a detailed examination of each of the three "classic" cases, and see what happens. Remember what is happening: an inserter is going to play a spot for a customer, and the spot *must* be present on the inserter.

Case 1:

A leaf inserter must play spot S. Either that spot is already on that inserter or it isn't there.

1.a. The spot is there, so the leaf plays the spot, and everything is fine.

1.b. The spot is *not* there, and so we proceed to the second case.

Case 2:

The leaf inserter "asks the portal" for the spot. This request is called an "NSR"; its form enables the portal to be efficient in doing its work.

Now, by consulting all the NSRs, the portal is able to decide which situation we have: *either* the spot is somewhere in that headend (either the portal or some other leaf has the spot), *otherwise* the spot is not at that headend.

2.a. The spot is already in some other inserter of this headend. The portal then *copies* the spot from the inserter which has it to the inserter needing it, thus producing the same state as 1.a, so the leaf plays the spot and everything is fine.

2.b. The spot is *not* anywhere in the headend, so we proceed to the third case.

Case 3:

The portal "asks HOME" for the spot. This request is called a "PSR" (which differs from an NSR); its form enables HOME to be efficient in doing its work. HOME is connected to the MASTER LIBRARY, so it can check to see whether the needed spot is there. Either the spot is in the MASTER LIBRARY, or it isn't.

3.a. The spot is in the MASTER LIBRARY. HOME then performs the transport of the spot (over the satellite) to the portal requesting it. Once the spot is on the portal, we simply proceed as in state 2.a. (Note that the portal also has to copy the spot to the needy leaf, since HOME can send spots only to portals.)

3.b. If the spot is *not* in the MASTER LIBRARY, the Operations department must be notified to deal with the situation.

At this point we now cross from the mechanical to the human realm. Subsidiarity is still occurring, though we are now talking about human departments within the company rather than clusters of connected machines. Indeed, in an appropriate paradox, it was at first not easy for us to see that these human interactions were still based on Subsidiarity. Eventually we learned why: since there are many complications which can arise, the details for the human stages are not as easy to describe as in the mechanical realm. Nevertheless, as you shall see it is still Subsidiarity.

Here is one possible phrasing of the fourth case:

Case 4 (and higher cases):
Operations is informed by the monitoring machinery, which shows all needed spots on the "To Be Encoded" list. Usually, the operator has a collection of tapes waiting to be encoded, probably including those which are in the list. Let us say he had been busy resolving another matter, and is now able to perform the encoding: He checks the To Be Encoded List and groups the available tapes according to what is being requested, then encodes them. The encoding machinery puts the spot into the MASTER LIBRARY, so that spot can now be handled mechanically by step 3.a above.

But perhaps the required tape is *not* present there. The operator then "appeals" to the Traffic department: "Where's the tape for spot 55506361?" Perhaps Traffic has the tape but were merely delayed in bringing it to Operations, so someone brings the tape over, and it is encoded, and again the work proceeds as in case 3.a above. Then again perhaps Traffic does *not* have the tape, so Traffic must then "appeal" to the Ad Sales department, which presumably could even "appeal" to the customer. Once we have gotten to the customer, of course, there cannot be any further appeal, for in that case he doesn't really have a spot to be played.[37]

So, as you can see, this layering (leaf, portal, HOME, Operations, Traffic, Ad Sales, customers) is strikingly similar to the "hierarchy" of assistants which Jethro proposed to Moses, and a nearly mathematical statement of Subsidiarity as described in the Papal documents.

The three levels, in non-tech language
This is the heart of my example, and I really want you to have a good picture. To help to clarify this, I will restate the above three levels using more abstract, generic terms:
1. An individual (Andy) has a job to do. Either (case a) he has all the resources to do it, or (case b) he doesn't:
    1.a. Andy *has* sufficient resources, so he performs his job.
    1.b. Andy *is lacking* something he needs, so we proceed to the second step.
    2. Andy appeals to *his* immediate superior (Bob), one level above. (Here,

---

[37] There is a subtlety here. One might say that the customer could "appeal" to the production house which had been hired to produce the video of the commercial. However, this has transcended the ad insertion system as we have described it, and is really another separate system with its own internal complexities. In a later chapter we shall consider the extension of Subsidiarity to such multiply overlaid systems, which are of course the predominant form of real human social organization.

I should note that this "superiority" is according to the particular job at hand, not necessarily according to any other measure of order either with respect to that individual, or within the system.)

Either (case a) Bob can render assistance to Andy, or (case b) he cannot:

2.a. Bob *can* satisfy the need, and does so, which permits Andy to proceed as in 1.a.

2.b. Bob *cannot* satisfy the need, so we proceed to the third step.

3. Bob must now appeal to *his* superior (Carl, who is an even higher authority, two levels above Andy) for assistance. We should observe that this appeal might *not* be identical to the appeal Andy made to Bob.

Again, (case a) Carl may be able to help, or (case b) he cannot:

3.a. Carl *can* satisfy the need, and does so, which permits Bob to proceed as in 2.a. (It is not formally essential that Carl helps Bob to the exclusion of Andy; indeed, Bob's request may require Carl's direct assistance of Andy.)

3.b. Carl *cannot* satisfy the need, so he must appeal to Dave in the next higher level.

And so on...

Obviously, in an abstract, or formal scheme of Subsidiarity, or in a practical form of application to real systems, there could be any number of levels, though sooner or later one comes to the "ultimate authority" in the system. In our example, this can easily be seen, for after the three levels I listed above, the need transcends the ability of the machinery to resolve, and so human intervention is required, which highlights the fact that the form of appeal can differ at each transition between the levels.

The three levels again, as a story, but with more technical detail.

In my struggle to present as much as I can to you, I will give you another version of the three levels, this time with additional detail. (After this, if you still want more technical detail, you can find it in an appendix.)

Somewhere in a distant headend, there is an inserter which happens to be a leaf. It is not the portal, so it cannot communicate directly with Headquarters. That inserter has just received a new schedule, saying that Marta's spot must be played on a certain network on a certain date and time. (Here, we're at step 1.)

That spot could be there, if perhaps Marta had closed the restaurant for remodelling, and requested her Ad Sales representative to stop its playback during the renovations. But as matters would have it, the spot is a new one (maybe she added some new items to her menu) so the machinery of the inserter determines that this spot is not already stored within its own disk drive. That inserter *needs help* if it is to ever get that spot. (Remember, this is an analogy.)

So the leaf appeals to its superior: it *sends a request* to its portal in the headend. This request is called the NSR or "needed spots request." It is just another computer file containing a two-part list: the spots already on the leaf, and the spots that it needs, because they are mentioned on the current schedule.

The portal collects these NSRs from *all* the leaves in the subtree (including itself, since it also is an inserter). In order to simplify the process, the portal also makes its own NSR because it is itself an inserter, and simply gives it to itself. So the program called FERRY running on the portal combines those lists, by which it will know all the spots which exist somewhere in the subtree, and also all the spots which are needed somewhere within the subtree.

(Here, we're at step 2.) The program called FERRY on the portal does what we call "subsidiarity" for the portal, which has two parts:

a. If there is a spot needed somewhere in the subtree which is already located somewhere else in the subtree, FERRY copies it from the place-where-it-is to the place-where-it-is-needed. This saves lots of time and effort if the spot is already at the headend.

b. FERRY makes a list of ALL the spots needed somewhere in the subtree which are *not* located *anywhere* in the subtree. This list is called the PSR (for Portal Spot Request) and that list is sent back to our Headquarters to the computer called HOME.

But, remember we said that this spot for Marta is a *new* spot, so the request goes back to HOME.

Back at our Headquarters on HOME, the program called PUMP collects the PSRs from all of the portals. (Perhaps you can see the parallel here? PUMP on HOME is like FERRY on the portal; PUMP collects PSRs from the portals, FERRY collects NSRs from the leaves.)

Note that these are requests for needed spots, not lists of existing spots. Also note that a portal cannot send spots to another portal – there is no arrangement for that in the satellite network. Rather, PUMP combines all the PSRs, then compares them to the current spots in the MASTER LIBRARY.

(Here, we're at step 3.) So PUMP then does what we call "subsidiarity" for HOME, which requires the making of two new lists:

a. The "To Be Sent" List: any spot appearing in some PSR and found in the MASTER LIBRARY.

b. The "To Be Encoded" List: any spot appearing in some PSR but *not* found in the MASTER LIBRARY.

Both lists are put into an order based on the urgency of the spot need. Then PUMP uses the "To Be Sent" list to send out the spots – one of the advantages of the VSAT network was that we could perform a *multicast* by which (in one step) we could send a spot to all of the portals which needed that spot. Meanwhile, as those spots are being sent out, the "To Be Encoded" List is displayed on a screen which is monitored by the Operations Department, and that "request" will be dealt with as their work load (and other resources) may permit.

The *Third* Level – and More

So you see there are *three* levels. Remember, in the ancient Roman army, Subsidiarity was accomplished by the *triarii* – the *third* level of defences? A leaf can ask the portal for a spot it needs. The portal can ask HOME for a spot it needs. HOME can ask the Operations department for a spot it needs. Here I might mention one of the practical details of our real system: the "To Be Encoded" list was organized according to the urgency, or priority, of when the spots were needed, and this enabled Operations personnel to arrange their work more effectively.

Obviously, any given spot on the To Be Encoded list may not be available for Operations to encode. Generally speaking, one may consider this to the fourth level of Subsidiarity, in which Operations appeals to Traffic for the tape, perhaps because Traffic had not yet delivered the tape to Operations. However, there are other reasons, some of which are definitely not easy to resolve. For example, the customer may not have brought the tape to Traffic. Or the tape may be there under a different number, because that spot id had been mistyped when it was entered into the Traffic-and-Billing program. Or, in some ways a more serious problem, the tape had been available, but it was defective in some way, so it could not be encoded. Such things cannot be solved mechanically, and clearly the human element in Operations must now take action.

Speaking in general, there usually are higher levels. (Three is merely notable because the ancient term indicated the *third* level of soldiers, as we mentioned in our introduction.) In fact, as you have seen in the preceding diagrams, our example could actually be said to have seven:

1. leaf
2. portal
3. HOME
4. Operations
5. Traffic
6. Ad Sales
7. customers.

Other systems may have more or fewer levels, depending on the need.

Chapter 4
OPAL – the Key to Subsidiarity

So now that I have thoroughly confused you with an explanation of how cable TV plays commercials for local businesses, I will try to clarify the picture. Not so much about cable TV, but about Subsidiarity and its application to this problem. To do this, I will have to specify the basic points by which Subsidiarity is defined, It would be more exciting to list those points at the end, as in a detective story, but it will be far more clear to put them first, and *then* explain how they relate to our example.

As we noted in the introduction, Subsidiarity is something which applies to the workings of a system or organization, or organism, and the fundamental character of Subsidiarity is *orderly assistance* in the working of that system. What is implied by such a foundation? It seems that we might consider four major facets:

(1) **Order**. There is some kind of arrangement of the organization aimed at reaching a certain goal, and the parts of that organization are arranged into a number of layers or departments of action.

(2) **Purpose**. There is some kind of primary objective or major goal which is to be accomplished by the organization.

(3) **Ability**. The nature of that goal requires the performance of a *variety* of tasks.

(4) **Limitation**. There are inherent difficulties which will be encountered in the work towards that goal.

Purpose

One of the Latin bits I learned from my mother was the motto of her high school, *Dic cur hic* : "Tell why (you're) here." That is, know your purpose. The topic of *purpose* is by far the most volatile and arguable of our points, for whole philosophies are set up to argue bitterly against the possibility of *purpose* in the real world, especially when one links *purpose* with *science*, specifically, with *evolution*. And yet purpose has a powerful appeal to the intellect:

> Few features of existence seem to point so effectively to a cause beyond them as is their appearance of being designed for some purpose.[38]

This excerpt is from the introduction to an entire volume devoted to an exploration of *purpose*, and to providing some background and distinctions touching the branch of philosophy called *teleology* or the study of "ends" or purposes, and its relation to science. Because some people miss the paradox, particularly when dealing with evolution, Jaki writes:

> Clearly, the Darwinist flouting of purpose can issue in grim prospects, in addition to presenting one with that primarily academic spectacle which is best rendered by Whitehead's

---

[38] S. L. Jaki, *The Purpose of It All*, ix

inimitable remark: "Those who devote themselves to the purpose of proving that there is no purpose constitute an interesting subject for study."[39]

While the philosophers and academics continue their purpose of getting more journal articles written and published, even ones denying the reality of purpose, the real corporate world of industry knows better. The first point we learn from our cable TV example is the lesson well-known to those in industry and lost to so many in academics. There must be a *purpose* underlying the investment of time, materials, and human effort; there must be some fruits, according to the nature of the industry. Speaking very generally, in a typical company one cannot start a project just from personal – or theoretical – interest. Even more so when the industry is directed to a specific end: and I am not talking about money. Money is the result of achieving that end, and not the end in itself, otherwise we would all be robbing banks. Yes, contrary to the phrasings of the all too common cheerleaders from schools of management, the purpose of the typical company is *not* to make money. It is to perform whatever service or make whatever product that company provides. Unlike the purposeful journal-article-writing anti-teleologist, however, there is no paradox here, because the company knows that the performance of the service or making of the product causes the earning of profit, and the paying of employees.

Now, the primary purpose of the cable TV industry is to supply the viewing public with various television networks. As a result of the geographical division of that supply, and other technical issues, this arrangement provides an opportunity for local advertising – that is, to perform insertion of local spots tied to geographical areas. So, because the primary purpose was already being achieved, a secondary purpose arose, that is, as many local spots as possible are to be played according to the requests of the advertisers (limited by the rules of the networks, availability etc.) This purpose of *local ad insertion* is the driving force of the entire system I have described at length. Obviously, as in every other human activity, problems occur from time to time: errors, oversights, mistakes, even malicious acts. But all the actions of the company are directed towards that central purpose: playing as many spots as possible, according to the customer requests and the inherent limitations of the system.

Order

Order is perhaps the aspect most deeply associated with the "military" origin of Subsidiarity, and though it is the most obvious of these aspects, it is also the most elusive. For order is nothing more than the idea that things are arranged in a "right relation" to each other. What the specific order may be depends on what those things are (and there may be a variety of specialized forms), and what the ultimate Purpose is – so it requires wisdom to

---

[39] S. L. Jaki, *The Purpose of It All*, 57, quoting A. N. Whitehead, *The Function of Reason* 12

understand how to arrive at those "right relations." By this term, Order, I mean the concept of System in its largest sense, which must involve Purpose: things which are *placed together*, not just adjacent. If the purpose was sports, we would call it a team; if music, an orchestra or band; if industry, a company or corporation; if food, a restaurant, or at least a kitchen. But I want to avoid the sense of order portrayed in the all-too-common "org chart" which is the usual diagram of representing a company's organization. Any non-trivial collection of things, especially if those things are called an "organization" or "organism," can usually be "organized" according to a number of different rules, and the sense of these terms suggests "working together" (the Greek *ergon* means work): yet the rule often used in companies is the rule of "power" – that is, who reports to whom. Such relations may be demanded for certain corporate legalities, but they are rarely relevant to the Purpose. For example, it is possible to know what organs are above, below, to the left and to the right of, say, the heart – but what matters more is the organs it is connected to, or functions with – for that is what accomplishes (or fails to accomplish) the Purpose.

The diagram of Order might be called a *teleological* diagram, for it shows how the Purpose is accomplished by the various abilities or specializations within the organization. For mechanical components, the order is clearly indicated by the wiring, plumbing, conveyor belts, networking, programming, or even by the physical location which joins one such component to another – again, however, according to the nature of the Purpose, not simply for the sake of a map, or other incidental linking. For human components, the order arises from instructions or habits: the rules of the game, standing orders, department protocols, or corporate policies, from code or treaty or tradition or custom or doctrine: that is, from any of the ways in which humans arrange their cooperation.

One may, in any case, devise a certain kind of "Abstract Subsidiarity." (I have given a rough form of it in an appendix.) The general idea is not very difficult to understand, providing one thoroughly banishes any idea of an "org chart" from the mind. As we saw in our chapter on history, the idea was sketched out by Jethro in his suggestion to Moses (Ex 18:21-22) about how to lessen his work load by assigning others to deal with the simpler cases. The lowest level of the organization deals with the Purpose in its most direct, or simplest sense. The second level deals with issues of low complexity, whenever the task exceeds the abilities of the individual in the first level. The third level likewise assists the second, and so forth, throughout the system, each level having a higher authority to whom appeal is made in case of need. Such a layered approach is very well-known in computing and in other fields of study: it is called the "tree-structure" or hierarchy. Note that the tree is inverted from its usual appearance in nature: our arrangement has the leaves at the bottom, and as one ascends in the structure, there are an ever-diminishing number of branches, merging finally into the "trunk" (usually termed the "root") which is the highest member in the organization. The drama here is that the system works inversely as usually considered by corporate politics: the lowest members are most important, and the higher members are there to serve the lower.

A friend of mine, Mike Kelso, who worked in the Field Services department, expressed the wrong way of structuring a system as "building a pyramid starting from the top." Subsidiarity means that the pyramid must be built starting with a solid foundation: the lowest level, which deals directly with the Purpose, is the *most important*, and (as if by Chestertonian paradox) all *the higher levels support the lowest level*, even though they are "above" it. When this order is not adhered to, all kinds of complications can arise, and the system will grow ever more complex as it diverges from the Purpose; in the end it is merely a self-interested parasite.

Though I have called this method a "tree-structure" or hierarchy, and these terms have very precise meanings in the mathematics of computer science, such a method can have a variety of extensions, or even distortions, once it is put into practice. As one ponders this hierarchical method of organization, one will also see another very curious fact about it. Since we are usually talking about real organizations, real companies, and so on, there may be multiple variations of this ordering, depending on which particular need or function one is considering: for certain needs perhaps a given individual must be consulted, while for certain other needs, someone else must be turned to. This is therefore joined to the two remaining topics, "abilities" and "limitation" which we shall discuss shortly.

In our exploration of ad insertion, we have seen the "right relation" of the entities involved. The various functional elements (departments or machines) are placed according to existing restrictions (such as the inserters at the headends) or convenience (the various departments at Headquarters). These elements are united by pathways according to the nature of their relation to each other: leaves connect to the portal by a computer network; Traffic can deal with Operations in person or by telephone or by e-mail.

But the important idea underlying all this is the idea of a hierarchy: there is a series of levels among which are communicated various needs and supplies. It is not in the abstract sense essential that the structure of a complex organization be literally hierarchical: there could be any form of interrelation which the Purpose requires, yet there should still be an underlying hierarchy forming the backbone of structure for cases of doubt or emergency.

Limitation

Like Purpose, it would be possible to write a whole chapter about Limits. (For example, see the title essay in Jaki's *The Limits of a Limitless Science and Other Essays*.) To acknowledge physical boundaries, limitations, and restrictions is not pessimistic but realistic: indeed, limits are some of the surest indicators of liberty. A limit is a paradox, and one which Chesterton mentioned time and again:

Art is limitation, the essence of every picture is the frame.[40]

A wall is like a rule; and the gates are like the exceptions that prove the rule. The man making it has to decide where his rule will run and where his exception shall stand. He cannot have a city that is all gates any more than a house that is all windows; nor is it possible to have a law that consists entirely of liberties.[41]

Has not every one noticed how sweet and startling any landscape looks when seen through an arch? This strong, square shape, this shutting off of everything else is not only an assistance to beauty; it is the essential of beauty. The most beautiful part of every picture is the frame. ...boundaries are the most beautiful things in the world. To love anything is to love its boundaries; thus children will always play on the edge of anything. They build castles on the edge of the sea, and can only be restrained by public proclamation and private violence from walking on the edge of the grass. For when we have come to the end of a thing we have come to the beginning of it.[42]

Certainly, limits are part of the essence of life in our world, and even when they are "an assistance to beauty," so often they definitely make things difficult. Severe restrictions exist in the physical world, despite the amazing creativity of human beings, and their concerted efforts, and continuing developments in many branches of science and technology, and even sufficient funding to accomplish the purpose at hand. And this is simply reality: since both humans and machines are finite beings, they are limited. There's only so much anyone can perform, only so much one can accomplish – and yet we feel the pull of eternity, and we cling to hope even in the most desperate situations. Though it sounds very theoretical, the ontological limitation of created beings is at the root of the limitedness we experience – and so Limitation is a completely *practical* consideration. Everyone can recognize that any machine can only move so much, or run so fast, or work so precisely, a container can only hold so much and then it overflows, one can only draw so much electrical power, and then the circuit blows; even when devices can be extended or replaced with a larger unit, there is always a certain "maximum" which limits its performance. So too with humans, in a certain, and particular sense: for example, physically, one can only lift so many boxes, type so many words, bypass so many hearts – and then one has to rest. But there are mental or other limits as well: one may be bound by the Order: the rules of the game, the corporate policy, or by mere practicality of things. There are other limits, relating to physics, like gravity, or physical realities, such as geography. Or even by the sheer contrariety of things: the customer may request something, then he changes his mind and leaves, for reasons that have nothing to do with you, your company, or anything else.

---

[40] GKC, *Orthodoxy* CW1:243
[41] GKC, *The New Jerusalem* CW20:229
[42] GKC, *Tremendous Trifles* 121-2, 146

(He may have forgotten his wife's birthday, perhaps, and wants to get to a flower shop before they close.)

It would be tedious, and lengthy, to list all the many limits faced in accomplishing local ad insertion. Some are not germane to our discussion, or at least are not involved in a direct sense. But some limits are critically involved, and it may be helpful just to mention a few.

1. The geographical division of the cable system. Since our purpose of ad insertion is secondary to the primary one of supplying networks to viewers, the cable company is not going to re-arrange the wiring of thousands of homes to suit local ad insertion. Other criteria apply which must take precedence, so ad insertion has to use what exists. So the division of the cable system into headends is a given, and ad insertion must conform, and adjust to any changes as the cable system develops.

2. The communication costs involved in getting spots to the given collection of headends. In an earlier day, the spots had to be stored in the form of tapes, and delivered to each headend by hand: that is, someone had to drive there, and actually install the tapes in the insertion machinery. At best, critical performance data (spot-logs and other monitoring) was retrieved by computers over the telephone line. In our particular case, a communication technique using a satellite was found to be cost-effective, compared to the slowness (and cost) of the older technique, or the much higher cost of a earth-based computer network (the "INTERNET"). It must be borne in mind that the transport of a typical spot (20 megabytes) is a much higher burden on a computer network than most files transported by typical home users of the INTERNET. Once the selection of a satellite transport technique was made, another set of limits were encountered.

3. Only *one* spot could be sent at a time, though it could go at once to as many headends as desired, with no additional cost. Related to this was the amount of time required to send out a spot: a rough estimate was to *double* the playing time of the commercial, so the most common 30-second spot would take around one minute to send to the Field.

4. Physical space at the headend was at a premium. The headends, already crammed full, were limited in what new equipment could be installed. Only one dish was permitted at each site – and for technical reasons that dish could be connected to only one computer.

5. The limits of the inserter itself. The computer only had room for up to eight network playback devices, so headends which needed support for more than eight networks required multiple inserters. Cost considerations limited the size of the disk drives required in each computer.

I must call your attention to these last two limits, for it was the combination of these which set the stage for the formulation of our file transport programs called PUMP and FERRY – and as we saw earlier, it was the parallel between (1) PUMP supplying the portals in the Field and (2) FERRY supplying the leaves of the subtree which set up the essential "three level" picture which we came to call "subsidiarity" for spot transport.

Ability or Specialization

As soon as one enters into almost any hobby or field of study, one begins to note the many possible branches of specialization for that field. One cannot delight in music without selecting this or that song or opus, and if one wants to perform, there are dozens of instruments to choose from. Likewise in art (painting in oils or water, or sculpture), or in cooking (Italian, or Mexican, or breakfast) or in writing (poems, or essays, or plays). Or sports (football, or bowling, or hiking). And if only I knew more about sports, I might be able to provide a wider discussion of this aspect of our topic. But there is the point I am trying to make: even though I "know" some basic differences between sushi or enchiladas, or linebackers and quarterbacks, or violas and drum kits, that does not mean I have the talents or training or skill or experience to deal with any of these varied specialities of human endeavor. It is a marvel as well as a challenge for us, especially as we "come of age" and select a career, to fit our abilities to the possible positions which may be available. And the same is true of hobbies as well. But the fact that the same man can play second bass in the local orchestra and shortstop in a local softball team suggests that humans have a strangely universal quality even as they specialize: he might be a great typer, a lousy cook, an honest man if sometimes quick-tempered, and yet he's important at work because he's been there for years and knows the place like the back of his hand.

As all this hints, Ability could be almost as large a topic as Purpose: indeed, it must be something mystical as it is hinted at by no less than St. Paul, in his explanation called "the Analogy of the Body":

> For as the body is one and hath many members; and all the members of the body, whereas they are many, yet are one body: So also is Christ.[43]

This verse, one of the most insightful and profound in the Epistles, stands at an important junction in the intellectual disciplines, and I will elaborate further when I discuss Subsidiarity and the body. For in trying to understand more about the body, I encountered the special branch of anatomy called *histology*: the study of tissues and cells, and the cataloging of the remarkably diverse "many members" of the living being. But one need not go very far into biology to learn the important differences between bone and muscle and blood and nerve, and see that the limits of one part are balanced by a talent of another part, and the many small specialities are united into a larger generality. Such purposeful differences in specialized function of the biological organism suggest that further study will be fruitful in unexpected ways, and not only for biology.

Ability or Specialization refers to the various components or aspects or details involved in the accomplishment of the Purpose: we might call these things "divisions and departments" when discussing a company, or "organs and tissues" in relation to living beings, or "tasks and subtasks" if we're trying to be abstract. This specialization, however, does not really arise from

---

[43] 1 Cor 12:12

the individuals involved, but from the purpose to be accomplished. Any given individual might be better or worse at a specific task, and in an example like ours, it is clear that training plays an important part. But the specialization must be understood as referring *first* to the accomplishment of the Purpose.

Considering our example of spot transport for cable TV, we can see that some tasks are strictly mechanical, and are most likely performed by machines, even though there will usually be a way of envisioning humans as performing such tasks. (In a later chapter I will reveal the secret behind my own case of software development.) Other tasks, just as obviously, can in no way be performed by machinery, and so will require specific human abilities, and all the usual arrangements which are required by such employment: human resources, payroll, a lunchroom, janitorial staff, etc. In the opening years of the 21st century, humanity has an amazingly vast array of tools and skills at its disposal to accomplish all manner of objectives. But it should be obvious that many of these marvels do not apply to the purpose of our example: no vehicular transportation is required, except for the trucks used by Field Services to take new or replacement inserters out to the Field. Our purpose, after all, relates to electronic information, so we shall require computers, computer networks and related apparatus, a satellite, satellite dishes, transmitting equipment, telephones, and such kinds of things. But it should also be clear that even these marvels are not mutually substitutable: one cannot use a telephone in place of a satellite dish, and a computer cannot be strung overhead along a hallway between two departments. There are a large number of specialized pieces of equipment which will be necessary. Even the computers, which are ready to run anything from games to word processing to DNA sequence analysis, must be programmed to do the various tasks of encoding or monitoring or insertion, and some of those programs require the addition of special components. This arrangement of mechanical tools requires not only an awareness of their individual functions, but also an awareness of their arrangement into the *system* which will accomplish the necessary tasks, in the proper manner and at the proper time. (This arrangement is done by another special department called "Development" which like Field Services is always on-call in order to deal with problems or emergencies.)

Turning from the machinery to the various departments, we see another kind of specialization in the various tasks performed by human beings. There is an interesting parallel here with the world of computers: unlike all other machines, a computer is, to a very large extent, a *general* tool which can be adapted to a vast range of uses, depending primarily on its *programming*. And though a computer may add faster than a human, a human being excels a computer in essential type, not in magnitude – even if one speaks merely in a pragmatic sense. (We're lots easier to program, for example.) And yet, at least in the industrial setting we are discussing, a human being can best perform those tasks he has been *trained* to perform.

Generally, then, when I speak of a *speciality*, I mean the training one has

39

according to the department where he works. (Obviously a person may be trained in multiple areas even if he is assigned to just one particular department.) For example, the people in the Traffic Department need to know things about the schedules and spot-logs, and how to control the software which deals with those things. The people in Field Services, however, have to handle the actual insertion machinery: they deal with wires and power, setting up of the dishes and the very special operation called "peaking" which is to align them so as to point directly at the satellite we used. The people in Operations need to know how to encode the spots, which means running the encoding equipment and reading the various audio and video level indicators; they must also understand the various monitors which report on the system status, and they serve as a first-level contact for Field Services and Traffic.

It will be clear that training of multiple people for the same duties provides an important benefit: that is, there will be replacements available if an individual is sick, on vacation, or otherwise unavailable. Here we should note that the divisions at the human level into departments are echoed in the lower mechanical level in the various "departmental" arrangements: the Home Cluster, the transport machinery, and the various subtrees in the Field. It is clear that the machinery will have its specializations; the same is true, at least in a general sense, on the human level.

There is another analogy I wish to mention to shed further light on this important aspect of "specialization." That is the idea of a sports team. Let us take a typical football team, with a head coach, offensive and defensive coachs, an offensive team with ends and quarterback, and a defensive team with linebackers, and the various special teams and positions, but there are also a number of others – medical staff, assistants for training, equipment, records, and so on – I need not list them; you may know them far better than I do. And perhaps you will also know all the various specialized physical, mental, and other skills needed by these various persons, both on the Field and on the sidelines. Yet, they are united in accomplishing one single purpose: winning the game. (Indeed, this may be a useful analogy which could greatly strengthen the argument of my book, but I do not have enough football knowledge to do it justice.)

So, just considering our example from a very high, almost casual level, we see certain specialized tasks – but we also begin to see the arrangement into human and mechanical departments, and get some hints as to the finer details of the necessary tasks to be performed. The challenge in listing the required tasks is to keep the Purpose in mind, but there is something more, which is why we speak of these tasks or departments being *organized*, or being *ordered* parts of a *system*.

A Summary

So if we are going to talk about an application of Subsidiarity to an organization, we need to consider four things: the ultimate *Purpose* of that organization; the real *Limitations* inherent in the work to be done; the

Abilities or specializations required (whether mechanical or human) in order to do the work, and the *Order* which arranges all the components into a complete unit which accomplishes that original purpose.

Subsidiarity enters into this picture in the one place where there is the possibility of improvement – indeed, the *only place* where it is possible to make any real alteration at all. Subsidiarity cannot change the Purpose, cannot abolish Limitations, nor augment Abilities, but Subsidiarity can adjust the *Order* in which the system is arranged. This new "Order" will be, in some fashion, a "layered" or "tree" arrangement, just as Jethro explained to Moses. Such an arrangement is really an extension or elaboration of the Order already necessary within the System or Organization being discussed, acknowledging the Limits and also the Abilities, and joining them effectively to achieve the Purpose. But since we are considering a real, specific case, we are now able to *see further* into the details of that extension.

Chapter 5
The Heart of Subsidiarity

Isn't Something Missing?

That phrase *seeing further* with which I concluded the last chapter should hint that I have neglected to mention something important in that discussion. You may have noticed that several times I have stated things like, "the leaf *appeals* to the portal" or "HOME *appeals* to the Operations department." There is one other element which must *join* the four components of Order, Purpose, Abilities and Limitations into one, the thing which is the whole *heart* of Subsidiarity. That is the idea of *Communication*.

As I have described our system, we have seen four different major forms of communication, four pathways each transmitting its own type of message:

1. From a leaf to its portal: the request, called an NSR, is a computer file containing both the spots on hand and the spots needed by that leaf. It is transported through the local computer network of the subtree.

2. From a portal to HOME: the request, called a PSR, is a computer file containing only spots needed by any inserter within the subtree. It is transported over the satellite pathway.

3. From HOME to the Operations department: the request is made visible by WATCHER, displaying the To Be Encoded list from PUMP. Because of the varying workload, and for a number of other reasons, Operations can only respond as permitted by the availability of the tapes, encoders, time to do encoding, and so forth. Obviously there are times when that list will only indicate spots needed in the future; knowledge of the system (either direct or indirect, which we shall explore shortly) would indicate whether that list needs to be monitored actively or not. (In just a moment we shall see more on aspects of the communication between the machinery and the operators.)

4. From the Operations department to the Traffic department: obviously this may be accomplished by e-mail, by telephone, or the operator might simply walk over to the other department. And during normal business hours, personnel from Traffic are often in the Control Room to deliver tapes or discuss issues. In a friendly environment, a large number of kinds of communications can be handled, and responded to, with minimal formality, but even then, certain protocols or standard practices remove unintended bumping or possible confusion points: for example, spot ids were to be written on paper, or sent by e-mail, in order to avoid transposition when transcribing them verbally.

Keeping Watch Over the System

It is not to be presumed that a need is going to be addressed unless the need is known: first, by the one experiencing the need, and second, by the one who is able to fulfill that need. So there must be various means of keeping the various components informed of the state of affairs. Obviously mechanical portions of a system will require a high degree of monitoring, but in the human realm, such communication does not mean some bizarre kind of "big brother" awareness of each individual action. It does, however, suggest a substantially better awareness than was shown in the parable of the Rich Man and Lazarus (Lk 16:19-31). Somehow there must be a certain natural awareness of the parts of the system. Again, we find our example providing us with details for our consideration.

When we first began serious discussions on the monitoring of the machinery which did the ad insertion, there were certain basic requirements which were obvious. (We already knew to provide a display showing the "To Be Encoded" list which we mentioned earlier.) We had to know whether the various computers were running, and that there was enough free space on the various disk drives for the work to proceed. We needed to have this information for the machinery at Headquarters as well as for the machinery in the Field. Remember that this had some specialized needs: the Field was organized by headends, but there were roughly three times as many inserters as headends. Also the portals had to pass along any information about the leaves at that headend, since the leaves had no other way of communicating with Headquarters. But remember that we are using this satellite connection to maintain contact between our Headquarters and all the portals of the Field: what if that pathway fails somehow? (Indeed, there were interferences possible from both natural and human causes.) So there had to be some way of knowing whether we were *still receiving* a signal from the machines in the Field. And we needed to know whether the program itself was still running, and not just sitting idle, pretending that everything was OK.

So, as we talked about monitoring as performed by workers such as air traffic controllers and 9-1-1 operators, military sentries and police or fire departments, we also recalled the Vestal Virgins of ancient Rome who kept burning the sacred fire, and that suggested the famous question from Juvenal's Sixth Satire: *Quis custodiet ipsos custodes?* – Who will watch the watchers themselves? He wondered how someone could ever come to have trust, as it would be clearly impossible to hire watchers, and watchers to watch them, and others to watch *them*, and so on. Hence the point as we applied it was this: how do *we* know that things are working correctly?

Part of the problem was straightforward. We arranged that each inserter produce a signal called the "heartbeat" which was sent to Headquarters on a periodic basis (about every 3 minutes). It was a packet of information about the machinery status, including how much free disk space the inserter had, and other basic facts about its work. Then a program was written which would display this information in a "tell-tale" – a colored spot of light, one for each headend. A green dot indicated that everything was working properly; other colors indicated various kinds of problems or failures. A timer was arranged so that the tell-tale would turn red if too much time went by without a heartbeat from the corresponding headend. As the primary users, the Operations department gave many helpful recommendations to Development, and the new tool was soon performing well. Eventually only two issues remained: First, how to make sure that the program was not faking us out with all green dots saying "everything is fine" ? Second, what to call the program?

So, being a Juvenal delinquent, I took that famous, nearly 2000-year-old Latin epigram, and put it in the corner of the screen – yes, in Latin – and arranged that every 15 seconds, it would alternate with other epigrams, (some of which are listed in the Glossary) or the company logo; after 9/11/2001, I added the American flag to the alternation. The continual change told the casual viewer that the program was running, and not idling. And the program name? Well, Juvenal solved that too: we called it WATCHER, so when people asked what the Latin quote meant, the translation had a special meaning for the Operations department, who then could explain "Who watches the WATCHERS?" by answering "We do." (Based on my own experience and on the performance over the 5.5 years the system was running, the trust was well-placed.)

Other Kinds of Appeal

A few pages back, we saw that there were four kinds of appeal, crossing between five successively higher levels of the organization; we noted that each of these varied forms were directly related to the primary satisfaction of getting a spot to the place where it plays. But now that we have seen other forms of awareness between the levels, we need to consider what other kinds of appeal there could be. This exploration can help to enlarge your view of the application of Subsidiarity, for it is easy to overlook certain trivial but disastrous cases: it is not just the lack of a spot which can fail to attain the Purpose: the machinery itself could fail, or be somehow prevented from doing its work.

For example, what happens when someone working in the headend accidentally disconnects the power from the inserters, and is not even aware that he did so? Soon, the heartbeat timer will expire, and the indicators will go red. The operator becomes aware of this by means of a WATCHER display in the Control Room; he follows a protocol to look into what could have gone wrong. The portal might have failed, the small satellite dish could have been bumped, the wire from the portal to the dish could have been disconnected, the power might have failed, there could be a local heavy snowfall; someone might be sitting in a nearby truck loafing with a radar detector turned on. (Yes, all these actually happened to us.) If he is unable to resolve the problem by means of the telephone, he calls for a special resource – the on-call member of the Field Services department, who will drive to the headend and repair or replace any damaged machinery.

Another Path to Knowledge

There was something else we did. For a long time, we did not recognize that we had actually done something innovative, and certainly did not connect it with anything already being done. But just as we took the idea of a "heartbeat" from physiology, we eventually found that we had built something reminiscent of another idea from biology. This idea is called *anastomosis*, and refers to the cross-linking which occurs between branches of arteries, or veins, providing alternative pathways for blood in case of temporary normal blockage (as can happen when certain joints are bent) or even in abnormal complications. The idea (as we apply it) is the broad awareness that *any* particular information one acquires can carry *additional* information implied even by the mere fact of that information being received. This information is often *inferential* but still helpful in knowing about the situation at hand. Such a cross-linking was not always planned for directly, but with an awareness of the larger structure of the system, its inherent opportunities can readily be put to good use.

For example, the reception of the PSR from a portal tells us that portions of the machinery are still functioning, even if we have (for some reason) not received a heartbeat. Even more strange would be the case where we are getting heartbeats from the other leaves, but not the portal; this might merely indicate that there is a mismatch between the configuration of the portal and the configuration at Headquarters.

In situations involving a human system, such "indirect" knowledge hints that there are ways of permitting certain information to be made known while preserving the necessary respect for human rights and dignity. It would hardly be appropriate to use Subsidiarity as an opportunity to usher in a "big brother" monitoring by the State! Indeed, it would be most unreasonable to use Subsidiarity to intrude into one's private life or home, particularly at the family level; this was the fundamental point Leo XIII stressed in the 1891 encyclical which gave rise to Subsidiarity in the modern sense. This is a serious matter, and needs to be examined.

The Negative Part Keeps Things Right

You may recall from our Introduction that Leo XIII's discussion of the idea of Subsidiarity, and in fact much of its early discussions, were phrased in a *negative* manner: "To desire, therefore, that the civil power should enter arbitrarily into the privacy of homes is a great and pernicious error."[44] In particular the standard reference in *Quadragesimo Anno* should be recalled:

> ...it is an injustice, a grave evil and a disturbance of right order for a larger and higher organization to arrogate to itself functions which can be performed efficiently by smaller and lower bodies. This is a fundamental principle of social philosophy, unshaken and unchangeable... [45]

I recall this negative view because it is the security against an over-application of a scheme of "communication" which would suggest that *anyone*, even if truly a "higher superior," can act in a direct manner when a need arises at a lower level. Our spot transport example might be custom-built to provide important counter-examples and justifications, showing the dangers and faults of such attempts as well as the just and correct uses of communication.

---

[44] *Rerum Novarum*, 21.
[45] *Quadragesimo Anno*

I must stress again that the "hierarchy" upon which Subsidiarity relies is *not* that of power, or control, or authority, according to the way in which these terms are often used in industry or government. Unfortunately, I should say, because the hierarchy of such organizations *ought to* conform to the Purpose of those organizations, and not to some merely social or political power struggle. (Remember: the pyramid must be built from the bottom.)

Let us start with one of the most stark situations: an inserter has failed. On the big screens of the Control Room, the corresponding tell-tale shows red, and Operations has done everything possible by means of the telephone. It is clear that someone will have to go to the headend to look into the failure, either repairing or replacing the failed component. But say someone from Traffic has just come into the Control Room to drop off a tape to be encoded. He looks up at the big screen and sees the red indicator: it is visible to anyone, but its meaning is not necessarily obvious, and even an operator must do some elementary research to know what is being reported by the signal. The Traffic coordinator cannot simply jump into his car and drive to that headend. Chances are that he will not only have no idea where the headend is located, but even assuming he knew that, and was somehow able to get inside once he got there, he would doubtless have no knowledge of how to repair the failed inserter. In fact, no one in Operations or any other department would know how to deal with such a failure, except for the Field Services department, whose job is to deal with such failures. (They are also authorized to use company trucks, they know the location of headends, and have other related information and abilities.) Here, we see the junction of limitation and specialization, but bounded or perhaps I should say controlled to a certain extent by the nature of the communications path. Certainly anyone in the Control Room could detect an abnormal signal (there were audible signals which were in fact made to be noticed) but in general only the Operations department were *authorized* to deal with such signals, at least as a first-level response.

For a completely different view, consider what might happen when a customer calls in to the Control Room to complain that he saw his spot running on the wrong network. The operator can do nothing more than take the information and report it to Ad Sales or Traffic; he has no authority to change the schedules, and in fact does not have access to the "Traffic and Billing" software which could make such an adjustment.

Next, let us consider the situation in which a leaf requires a certain spot, and it does not exist within the subtree. The portal receives the NSR request, but it cannot decide to refuse to pass on the request as a PSR to HOME. Granted, the portal is a machine, and has no free will. But there is a deeper sense to this example. The portal, having been appealed to according to the nature of the system, must fulfill that need, or else pass on the appeal, honestly and timely, and without prejudice to the requestor. And when it receives something it has requested for another, it must be passed on in a fully disinterested manner. Certainly this point is easy to understand when the components are machines, but the *same* virtues are required from the

46

humans within the system.

Protection for the Machinery

One of the most severe and perhaps most important of the restrictions in our system was the safeguarding of the production machinery: *no human was able to cause any direct alteration of the functions and behavior of any part of the machinery*, from HOME through the satellite pathway, out to the portals and the leaves: neither from Ad Sales nor from Traffic, not Operations nor Field Services – notwithstanding that all these departments have a "higher" rank according to the Order within the structure I have outlined. (This might be an even stronger exemplification of Subsidiarity, perhaps even more than the idea of "appeal" for spot transport.)

Although all these departments had a greater or lesser awareness of how the system operated (and certainly the technical departments had to have a substantial knowledge of its inner working), none of them could alter that operation by any means except in the manner permitted to their departments. There were two very special exceptions.

1. Operations had the ability to wipe out a spot everywhere throughout the Field, and in the MASTER LIBRARY: this was used if a spot had been encoded erroneously, or if the customer had given orders to cancel the showing of a spot.

2. Under emergency conditions, as determined by appropriate authority, other actions could be undertaken; these were either performed by, or directed by the Development department, the only department having full details of the pathways within the machinery.

I should also note that the prohibition did not include certain actions (typically involving Field Services and Operations) relating to installation or replacement of inserters and some other well-defined activities.

Despite these exceptions, this remarkable restriction deepens the divide between the human realm and the mechanical one. It should be recalled that there are a number of points of contact: the WATCHER program shows the current state of the machinery; the operators perform encoding, which bring new spots into the MASTER LIBRARY; the Traffic Department sends out new schedules and processes the returned spot-logs; Field Services performs a variety of functions on the inserters. But even in this last case, there was no direct alteration of the pathways – not even in the most severe task they could perform, the installation of a new inserter, when the disk drive was completely empty and there were no spots at all for the inserter to play. For once it had its schedules, the machinery took care of everything else. Anyone who watched this taking place could not help but be impressed as "subsidiarity" was invoked and all the necessary spots were delivered to it – typically it was busy performing ad insertion after a few minutes.

Thus, we have seen that the "negative" form of Subsidiarity, which as stated prohibits a higher level from undue meddling with the working of a lower level, also clarifies and strengthens the position of communication, the pivot of Order, within the system. In human terms, this requires virtues such as accuracy, honesty, humility, and a control over curiosity, as well as obedience and a concern for others.

Part III
A Glance at Three Other Examples

Chapter 1
A Glance at the University

"...liberal education, viewed in itself, is simply the cultivation of the intellect, as such, and its object is nothing more or less than intellectual excellence."

Newman, *The Idea of a University*, 145

Now that we have looked at how a company once accomplished ad insertion for cable TV, and considered an abstraction of a system which has Order, Purpose, Ability, and Limitation, with a variety of Communication pathways to give help but prevent undue interference, we shall briefly examine some other systems where Subsidiarity can (or does) play a role.

My title for this section emphasizes the University, but this argument applies to education in general, because the idea of education is in its simplest a direct application of Subsidiarity: the student appeals to his superior, the teacher, to supply his lack of knowledge:

If I want to know the volume of a cylinder I can, if I know how, work the problem out either by mathematics or by experiment: or I can ask a competent person to tell me what its volume is. In the last case I proceed on the lines of authority, and, in doing so, I convince myself first of all by an act of reason that my authority is a reliable one. This is only doing what every man of business does time and again in the conduct of his affairs.[46]

When your father told you, walking about the garden, that bees stung or that roses smelt sweet, you did not talk of taking the best out of his philosophy. When the bees stung you, you did not call it an entertaining coincidence. When the rose smelt sweet you did not say "My father is a rude, barbaric symbol, enshrining (perhaps unconsciously) the deep delicate truths that flowers smell." No: you believed your father, because you had found him to be a living fountain of facts, a thing that really knew more than you; a thing that would tell you truth to-morrow, as well as to-day. And if this was true of your father, it was even truer of your mother...[47]

A child, of course, cannot voice all the proper appeals, as a student might seek for the volume of a cylinder, but his parents understand even his wordless cries as appeals. The first thing they give must of course be language, which is the clue to the deep truth of Chesterton's epigram, "Free speech is a paradox"[48]: that freedom is gained only after years of training, the

---

[46] Windle, *The Catholic Church and Its Reactions with Science*, 52
[47] GKC, *Orthodoxy*, CW1:360
[48] GKC, *Robert Browning*, 174

49

slow building of the sense of hearing, the fine control of the organs of speech, and further years for the priceless gifts of learning to read and write – all of which is too easily forgotten in adulthood.

Of course education in itself cannot be simply the adult's reflex response to the innumerable questions of a child[49] – education must be orderly, and it must be universal. This applies *a fortiori* when we come to the structured arrangements of higher education, where we see the application of Subsidiarity.

As we mentioned in the introduction, in the 1850s Cardinal Newman wrote *The Idea of a University* to give his thoughts on the nature of the university, and how it should be structured. Though he stressed the proper handling of one particular subject (theology), the point can be made about *any* subject:

It will be said, that there are different kinds or spheres of Knowledge, human, divine, sensible, intellectual, and the like; and that a University certainly takes in all varieties of Knowledge in its own line, but still that it has a line of its own. It contemplates, it occupies a certain order, a certain platform, of Knowledge. ... I cannot so construct my definition of the subject matter of University Knowledge, and so draw my boundary lines around it, as to include therein the other sciences commonly studied at Universities, and to exclude the science of Religion. For instance, are we to limit our idea of University Knowledge by the evidence of our senses? then we exclude ethics; by intuition? we exclude history; by testimony? we exclude metaphysics; by abstract reasoning? we exclude physics. Is not the being of a God reported to us by testimony, handed down by history, inferred by an inductive process, brought home to us by metaphysical necessity, urged on us by the suggestions of our conscience? It is a truth in the natural order, as well as in the supernatural. ...

How can we investigate any part of any order of Knowledge, and stop short of that which enters into every order? All true principles run over with it, all phenomena converge to it; it is truly the First and the Last. In word indeed, and in idea, it is easy enough to divide Knowledge into human and divine, secular and religious, and to lay down that we will address ourselves to the one without interfering with the other; but it is impossible in fact. Granting that divine truth differs in kind from human, so do human truths differ in kind one from another. If the knowledge of the Creator is in a different order from knowledge of the creature, so, in like manner, metaphysical science is in a different order from physical, physics

---

[49] As Chesterton noted: The note of our age is a note of interrogation. And the final point is so plain; no sceptical philosopher can ask any questions that may not equally be asked by a tired child on a hot afternoon. "Am I a boy? – Why am I a boy? – Why aren't I a chair? – What is a chair?" A child will sometimes ask these sort of questions for two hours. GKC *George Bernard Shaw* CW11:483-4

from history, history from ethics. You will soon break up into fragments the whole circle of secular knowledge, if you begin the mutilation with divine. ... To blot it out is nothing short, if I may so speak, of unravelling the web of University Teaching. ... if you drop any science out of the circle of knowledge, you cannot keep its place vacant for it; that science is forgotten; the other sciences close up, or, in other words, *they exceed their proper bounds, and intrude where they have no right.* ... a science which exceeds its limits falls into error. [50]

This has a sound suggestive of the "negative" definition of Subsidiarity. But is there a *system* here? Indeed, yes:

The human mind cannot keep from speculating and systematizing; and if Theology is not allowed to occupy its own territory, adjacent sciences, nay, sciences which are quite foreign to Theology, will take possession of it. And this occupation is proved to be a usurpation by this circumstance, that these foreign sciences will assume certain principles as true, and act upon them, which *they neither have authority to lay down themselves, nor appeal to any other higher science to lay down for them.* For example, it is a mere unwarranted assumption if the Antiquarian says, "Nothing has ever taken place but is to be found in historical documents;" or if the Philosophic Historian says, "There is nothing in Judaism different from other political institutions;" or if the Anatomist, "There is no soul beyond the brain;" or if the Political Economist, "Easy circumstances make men virtuous." These are enunciations, not of Science, but of Private Judgment; and it is Private Judgment that infects every science which it touches with a hostility to Theology, a hostility which properly attaches to no science in itself whatever.

If then, Gentlemen, I now resist such a course of acting as unphilosophical, what is this but to do as men of Science do when the interests of their own respective pursuits are at stake? If they certainly would resist the divine who determined the orbit of Jupiter by the Pentateuch, why am I to be accused of cowardice or illiberality, because I will not tolerate their attempt in turn to theologize by means of astronomy? And if experimentalists would be sure to cry out, did I attempt to install the Thomist philosophy in the schools of astronomy and medicine, why may not I, when Divine Science is ostracized, and La Place, or Buffon, or Humboldt, sits down in its chair, why may not I fairly protest against their exclusiveness, and demand the emancipation of Theology? [51]

---

[50] Newman, *The Idea of a University*, 66-67, 103, 106; emphasis added.
[51] Newman, *The Idea of a University*, 124-5; emphasis added.

51

In case you are wondering about those names, La Place was a French astronomer and mathematician (d. 1827); Buffon was a French naturalist (d. 1788); Humboldt was a German scientist (d. 1859). Also, I must point out that Newman uses the word "science" to mean any discipline of orderly study, for the Latin *scientia* means *knowledge*. Clearly, a University is a *system* of *all* fields of study; each does its own work in pursuit of knowledge and of truth, but each works in its "own territory" in its own specialized manner and according to its own proper rules. *But* each field of study works in relation with the other fields: sometimes as an assistant or ally, as chemistry works with metallurgy, or literature with history; sometimes merely in that the same object is studied but under differing degrees or methods, as both geography and geology study the earth, or both history and anatomy study human beings; and sometimes as mere adjacency, as when both are housed in the same building, or are studied on the same day.

How, then, can Subsidiarity play a role in a University?

Such a discussion might easily fill an entire book. But our example assists us to make a start, which may suggest future explorations. First, we should note the basics about a University.

1. Obviously the Order does not mean the campus buildings, or the organization of departments under a provost. It may be nothing more than poetical, but I cannot give a better symbol than the diamond, which has countless facets, some larger, some smaller, each bordering on many others, and also reflecting many others.

2. Its Purpose for the student is the pursuit of knowledge; for the professor it is the dissemination of knowledge.[52]

3. Its Abilities (or specializations) are the various fields of study.

4. Its Limitations – hmm, a difficult item to describe. Let us say that the limitations are *also* the fields of study. For each field is constrained by its own structure or character: a voltmeter cannot measure rhyme.

So, indeed, we might begin to get a suggestion of what the true Order, and the necessary communication, must be. Each of the facets are *mutually subservient* to each other: any discipline (or team of disciplines) must be ready to assist as the explorations of another may require. If Truth be the purpose, no field *dare* permit the work of another to be usurped. Even if two facets do not seem to be neighbors, perhaps one must serve to reflect the Light – as (for example) History might mediate a conflict between Literature and Philosophy.

In such a system, the most important virtue to be exercised is *patience*. Different disciplines rarely share terminology, much less methodology; they

---

[52] Emphatically *not* the acquisition of "new" knowledge via research. Newman mentions this explicitly: "To discover and to teach are distinct functions; they are also distinct gifts, and are not commonly found united in the same person. He, too, who spends his day in dispensing his existing knowledge to all comers is unlikely to have either leisure or energy to acquire new." [Ibid., Preface]

do share the common pursuit of Truth. While this is remembered, strong *bridges* are built between the facets, and the diamond increasingly shines with Light.

But when the facets refuse to build such bridges, there is danger in the darkness.

Newman singled out Theology as the discipline which (in the 1850s) was getting "dropped out of the circle of knowledge." Even in the early 21st century, this still happens. But in some places, there is just as much danger to the "hard" sciences – broadly, all those which require mathematics, and which almost never have essay questions on tests – ranging from physics and chemistry, geology and astronomy, to all the branches of engineering. These are not simply usurped, but despised, or more often ignored, which is always safer, and easier to do, especially if one has no clue what all that math is about. It's just as dark to ignore the math as it is to ignore the Latin, when both things were devised to yield light and knowledge.

It is hardly impressive to see those theologians, philosophers, historians, and literary specialists using the INTERNET, or even typing up their latest journal articles with some word-processing software and running off copies on the department laser printer. But mathematics will still serve the physicists, who serve the chemists, and materials engineers, who serve the electrical engineers, who serve computer people... and let's not forget all the engineers who make the roads, and get the fuels, and build the cars, and the power plants, so you can get to your library and turn on a light and read your books... No, things are much worse than in Newman's time. It is bad enough for other fields to grab the intellectual territory of another. It is far worse to deny the good work of the other fields, while still parasitically profiting from their labors. And this criticism applies both ways: it is a very shortsighted view to think that the "math" side and the "words" side are all that far apart. This question is explored in a very famous children's book, *The Phantom Tollbooth*, where the Kingdom of Wisdom is divided into the domains of Words and Numbers, warring against each other. In that story, a young boy reveals to the opposing sides their real opposition, the Demons of Ignorance, who have never stopped in their work of destruction and antagonism. It is important for the various departments of the universities to learn this is no fictional fantasy to be ignored. It is a most important need of human civilization, and Chesterton himself pointed it out more than 100 years ago in an essay called "A Defence of Useful Information":

> ...perhaps the taste for shreds and patches of journalistic science and history is not, as is continually asserted, the vulgar and senile curiosity of a people that has grown old, but simply the babyish and indiscriminate curiosity of a people still young and entering history for the first time In other words, I suggest that they only tell each other in magazines the same kind of stories of commonplace portents and conventional eccentricities which, in any case, they

would tell each other in taverns. Science itself is only the exaggeration and specialization of this thirst for useless fact, which is the mark of the youth of man. But science has become strangely separated from the mere news and scandal of flowers and birds; men have ceased to see that a pterodactyl was as fresh and natural as a flower, that a flower is as monstrous as a pterodactyl. *The rebuilding of this bridge between science and human nature is one of the greatest needs of mankind.* We have all to show that before we go on to any visions or creations we can be contented with a planet of miracles. [53]

It is not without significance that I have used the word "bridge" earlier. In the cartoon version of *The Phantom Tollbooth* as the hero is entering the Realm of Words, he sees all things as built out of the words they are: clouds formed from a billowy word *cloud*, hills made from *hill* heaped upon *hill* and so forth: but he crosses a bridge which is made of the word *confidence*. That is the hint of the problem relating to the bridge, and to Subsidiarity: the University must work to *reacquire a trustworthy scheme of communication*, both to guard against dropping members out of the circle of knowledge, and to strengthen our forces against our real enemy, the Demons of Ignorance. Why should those who inhabit the kingdom of Wisdom stop learning, even if they are teachers?

---

[53] GKC, *The Defendant* 74-75, emphasis added

Chapter 2
A Glance at the Body

As a mammalian embryo advances through the stages characterized by cleavage, morula, blastocyst and germ layers, it satisfies all its metabolic needs by simple, diffusive interchanges with the fluid medium in which it is immersed. But as the embryo continues to gain size and begins to take form, a functioning circulatory system becomes necessary in order to make use of the required food and oxygen obtainable from the mother's blood. Hence it is that the heart and blood vessels are the first organ system to reach a functional state.

Arey, *Developmental Anatomy* 375

Although it was in most ways a mere analogy, I described ad insertion in rather lengthy detail because it was a *complete system*, very limited in purpose and structural detail, and these limits helped highlight some important points about Subsidiarity which may have gone unnoticed if I used a more abstract approach. The idea of a university which we examined in the last chapter is much vaster and more intricate than the ad insertion system; moreover, it is a human system, and so is subject to all kinds of complexities. Even if, as a practical matter, we have been struggling to bring about respect and cooperation among the various disciplines or fields of study (and this appears not to have been attained since Newman's time), at least our study of Subsidiarity has been illuminated, for we know a University is clearly intended to pursue the one single purpose of *knowledge* in all its facets.

In this chapter, we again take a limited topic, but this time we look at one of the most complex physical systems known: the human body. This analogy is not my own idea: it is an extension from St. Paul's very famous "Analogy of the Body":

For as the body is one and hath many members; and all the members of the body, whereas they are many, yet are one body: So also is Christ. ... For the body also is not one member, but many. If the foot should say: Because I am not the hand, I am not of the body: Is it therefore not of the body? And if the ear should say: Because I am not the eye, I am not of the body: Is it therefore not of the body? If the whole body were the eye, where would be the hearing? If the whole were hearing, where would be the smelling? But now God hath set the members, every one of them, in the body as it hath pleased him. And if they all were one member, where would be the body? But now there are many members indeed, yet one body. And the eye cannot say to the hand: I need not thy help. Nor again the head to the feet: I have no need of you. Yea, much, more those that seem to be the more feeble members of the body are more necessary. And such as we think to be the less honourable members of the body, about these we put more abundant honour:

and those that are our uncomely parts have more abundant comeliness. But our comely parts have no need: but God hath tempered the body together, giving to that which wanted the more abundant honour. That there might be no schism in the body: but the members might be mutually careful one for another. And if one member suffer any thing, all the members suffer with it: or if one member glory, all the members rejoice with it.

1 Cor 12:12, 14-26

The human body is an exceedingly complex and most well-ordered system, yet relying on very basic components and mechanisms. Given the vast amount of knowledge of the body we have acquired since advances such as the microscope, molecular biology, and DNA sequence analysis, it would seem natural to explore that new knowledge and see how much more we can apply to that analogy.

The body has long been divided into various components and even systems: the arm, the eye; the stomach and heart and brain; and this was already known to the ancients. So St. Paul was speaking with complete biological accuracy as regards the strictly natural side of his analogy. In nearly 2000 years, that accuracy has not been voided; rather it has become more intensely true. At a finer level the idea of a *tissue* (muscle, nerve, ligament, vascular) was devised to provide a finer grain to the list of specializations within the body. The use of the microscope (beginning in the 1600s) gave rise to the concept of the *cell* as the fundamental unit of living creatures. Vast progress in chemistry, beginning with Wöhler's synthesis of urea in 1828, and assisted in the 20th century by important developments in nuclear physics, began to explain the gigantic complexity of the living cell.

This work culminated in the amazing discovery that a single complex chemical holds the complete instructions for building and running the machinery of the cell. (This work in itself might provide a useful example in our study, for it was accomplished by the cooperation of several separate disciplines!) That chemical, called DNA, is a series of four small chemicals known by their initial letters (A, C, G, T) but arranged in a complex sequence, just as any book is a complex sequence built from the alphabet and punctuation.

Even now that we know the mechanism by which the information in the DNA produces a result in the proteins of the living cell, and that the complete *genome* for some species has been recorded (for humans this requires some 3,000,000,000 characters) we have only begun to study the relations between that vast code and all the larger machinery and systems which are based on that genome.

This genome, the complete instructions and blueprints for the living cell, has the same relation to life as the complete score of a symphony has to the music it represents: there are many performers, each of whom, by following his own particular part of the whole, produces a result immeasurably greater than either those performers, or the score. (Amazingly, that score contains a description of both the instruments and the performers, but we must leave such things for another study.)

One of the questions which is now being anxiously explored is how those various parts are specified in the score: how the DNA directs the formation of all the structures by which the cells specialize to form the various tissues, organs, and structures of the body. But in order to proceed, all these structures must be characterized and known.

At the highest level, this study is called *anatomy*, which considers the large-scale arrangements of parts within the body. Here we learn about bones and their arrangement into the skeleton, the muscles and ligaments, the digestive system, the heart and the blood vessels and the lungs, the brain and nerves, and all the rest. The very famous *Gray's Anatomy* contains over 1000 pages of detail, and is still merely an introduction to the subject.

More detailed than anatomy is the subject called *histology*, which organizes the kinds of *tissue* from which the various organs and structures are built, and the kinds of cells from which the tissues are built. Even deeper are the subjects of microbiology and molecular biology, which shares subject-territory with biochemistry.

Then, once we know something about what goes on in a living body, we will need to understand how it got to be that way. In order to understand how these structures are put together from the original fertilized egg, one must explore *embryology* and *developmental anatomy* which traces the growth from the single cell through its various stages until the final adult form of some one hundred trillion cells is reached. In fact, only by recourse to the developing fetus can sense be made of certain strange arrangements to be found in the adult body.

Purpose, Biology, and Computer Science

As I mentioned earlier, when I discussed the idea of Purpose, there is quite a bit of debate raging at the frontier between biology and philosophy. I find it very interesting since computer science shares some of that same frontier, and also because some of the discoveries glimpsed by biology have already been studied at great detail by computer science: I refer to the matter of strings and patterns of characters, and machines which work based on such things, and the even more complex topic easily summarized in the term *programming*. Like every other form of writing, programming is certainly directed by teleology: there is always a *purpose* in writing a program, even if it is not a correct program, or if it is incomplete or unsatisfactory or unstable. Again, the debate on Purpose is even more interesting to me because I witnessed the various stages of the development of the ad insertion system I described previously, and some of them bear striking resemblance to various idiosyncrasies I have learned from my reading of developmental anatomy. Remember, the foremost criterion in life is that once the system is "up and running" it must stay that way, and any changes must be accommodated with the system as it already is. This same criterion had to be maintained in our performance of ad insertion.

I have seen this strong design-relation previously: my doctoral work brought computer science to assist with certain problems faced by molecular biologists. I had been personally interested in this topic for some time, and as I have read anatomy, histology, and molecular biology texts, I have found plenty of ideas which I have put to use in my own software. But this is to be expected from studying such things, as Copernicus wrote in dedicating his *De Revolutionibus* to Pope Paul III:

The machinery of the world has been built for us by the Best and Most Orderly Workman of all.[54]

In order to see this order as it relates to Subsidiarity, I will confine myself to a very limited but critically important part of the human body.

The Circulatory System

Although the essential point of ad insertion was to play commercials, a major function of our system was *transport*. Given that the cable company already owned a number of distant headends, and that devices for ad insertion were available for installation there, there really was just one hard part: getting the spots delivered to those distant places. It is strange to report that one of the most important parts of the body is also all about *transport*: it is called the *circulatory system*. It has a network of pipes carrying blood: arteries flowing outward, capillaries which are the places of commerce where materials are traded, veins flowing inward, and a pump at the center called the heart. You probably already know that the blood brings oxygen and food to the cells, and carts away carbon dioxide and other wastes.

The fundamental individual in this system can be no other than the living cell, and the specializations which such a real system demands are described by the various studies of anatomy, histology, and cellular and molecular biology: limiting our consideration to the circulatory system, there are cells which are connective or structural, muscle cells, and the red blood cells which actually handle transport. The limitations are that a cell can only ever grow to a certain size; it has its own particular restrictions on its mechanical qualities (a muscle cell can only pull with so much force, etc.) and then there are other requirements such as the need for all cells of the body to be "within a certain distance" from a blood vessel in order that they be nourished by osmosis from the bloodstream. I will mention another limitation shortly. The order of the system is dictated by the three billion character DNA code which directs the building and management of the body structures. The purpose (in our limited view of things) is to supply a continuous stream of blood to every area of the body. The communication involved could be considered with respect to the development of the system (studied in developmental anatomy and related fields) which is a matter of the various growth-control and specialization-control enzymes governing the various tissues as they grow. Or the communication might be considered as the activities within the circulation of an adult: the maintenance of blood flow and the regulation of blood pressure during various activities. This is

---

[54] S. L. Jaki, *Science and Creation*, 260; see his note 78

somewhat better known, and I will give just a brief hint of how things work.

Note that there are other parts of the body involved, specifically the nervous system. Typically we think of nerves as either carrying signals from our senses to the brain (which are called *afferent*) or from our brain to the muscles (which are called *efferent*). But some afferent nerves carry "system status" information: there are special sensors such as the *carotid bodies* which monitor the blood pressure. Likewise, some efferent nerves carry "system control" information: controlling not only the heart itself, but also the muscular lining of the small arteries (the arterioles) which give system-wide control over the blood pressure in the regions of the body:

As long as the arterial pressure remains normal, each local tissue in the body can control its own blood flow by simply dilating or constricting its local blood vessels. This mechanism ... is the means by which each tissue protects its own nutrient supply, controlling the blood flow in response to its needs. Therefore, since the venous return to the heart is the sum of all the local blood flows through all the individual tissues of the body, all the local blood flow regulatory mechanisms throughout the peripheral circulation are the true controllers of cardiac output under normal conditions. ... the whole theory of normal cardiac output regulation is that *the tissues control the output in accordance with their needs.* Again, it must be stated that it is not the heart that controls the cardiac output under normal conditions; instead, *the heart plays a permissive role that allows the tissues to do the controlling.* The heart does this by always maintaining a permissive pumping capacity that is somewhat above the actual venous return...[55]

That sentence ends with the words, "that is, except when the heart fails." There are a number of limitations which can arise, such as managing sudden blood loss or shock. In such cases the nervous system can be overridden by certain control substances (adrenaline or epinephrine) which can control the system-wide blood flow by emergency means. Such details are still consistent with the greater purpose of the living body, which might be phrased "to stay alive as long as possible."

Alternate Pathways

Other limitations are not as life-threatening. One such limitation is revealed in an interesting detail of anatomy. It is common knowledge that the arteries go outward from the heart, starting with the trunk-like aorta, which branches like a tree into several large arteries going to the arms and head, then turns downward to supply the various internal organs before sending off two large branches to the legs. The arteries then divide into smaller and smaller branches, finally ending in the capillaries, at nearly microscopic size, which are just big enough for the red blood cells to fit through, and the place where nourishment is imparted to the cells of the body. Then the tree-like

---

[55] Guyton, *Textbook of Medical Physiology*, 276; emphasis added

character of the vessels runs backwards: the capillaries re-unite into tiny veins, merging into larger and larger veins, until the two great trunks of the vena cava re-enter the heart (one from below, one from above).

Here is the interesting detail. In some places, the branches do not merely divide: they come back together and re-unite. This re-connection is called an *anastomosis* and as you might expect, it provides an *alternate pathway* for the blood flow, so that if (for example) a joint is flexed, impeding flow through one pathway, another pathway will still be open. There are many such cross-connections, in fact other than the heart itself, very few blood vessels are completely essential. As we say at work, the circulatory system has few "single points of failure." Redundancy is not always possible in a given system, but it provides a major advantage when the system permits it.

Such details of the structure of just this one system urge me to add some brief comments on its development. One of the most amazing facts about the circulatory system is that it is the very first system to be made functional, because it is the key to all future growth. Before there is a transport system in operation, the cells of the growing human must rely on *osmosis* (that is, physical transport by a fluid, something like water seeping through a towel). The growing baby is barely 4 weeks old when some blood cells, a few simple tubes and a one-chamber pump are united and the heart begins to beat. Once that system is running, growth can proceed, for there is now a transport system which serves the rest of the body.

Even more marvellous, and impressive (for someone like me who had to maintain that 24/7 functionality of the Home Cluster!) is the fact that once the heart starts, it *never stops*, even though both the heart and other major parts of the system must go through a number of structural alterations on the way to adulthood. The very first form of the heart is a tube with two valves around one muscle-lined pumping chamber; the main vessels are simple tubes arranged in pairs, and there are connections through the umbilical cord to the placenta. As the baby grows, the heart-tube folds, the paired vessels grow, new valves are added, new lines sprout and new connections are formed, and some earlier ones disappear; the lungs grow and are added to the system. Finally at birth, the entire placental portion is shut off, and major pre-birth pathways are closed down as the lungs finally come on-line. Indeed, there are few events in life as dramatic as birth, and though unseen and for the most part unnoticed, the sheerly mechanical changes to the circulation at birth are among the most dramatic, speaking merely from the system perspective. All of which indicates that a well-designed system can be arranged to safely and seamlessly accommodate even the nearly incredible transition from one form of nourishment and respiration to another, totally different form. It may take more work at the design stage, and such transitions are never easy nor without risk, but the advantage of such flexibility in a system is tremendous.

Chapter 3
A Glance at the Church Sacramental

"The heart is the cause of circulation."
Kimber *et al., Anatomy and Physiology* 367

We have, in a glance which was far too short, attempted to see something about Subsidiarity in some technical aspects of the human circulatory system. If Subsidiarity can touch, even in a vague, suggestive manner, on the order within the human body, how much more, then, might it touch on what St. Paul explored? To proceed, let us look at one more aspect of this amazingly complex and well-designed system.

You may be surprised to learn of a curious arrangement in the circulatory system, which, as it is part of the body, requires nourishment as all of the other parts do. But even that has to be arranged: the heart itself is supplied with blood vessels (the coronary arteries), and all the larger veins and arteries themselves have smaller blood vessels to supply them with nourishment. These are called the *vasa vasorum*, the "vessels of vessels." This term reminded me of a title of the Pope, *Servus servorum Dei*, the Servant of the servants of God.

For as we have learned, the order arising from Subsidiarity is an upside-down order: the higher parts perform their work for the sake of the lower parts, which carry out the Purpose of the system, and this is nowhere better exemplified than in the Catholic Church. In this context, I refer to the hierarchy in its strictest sense – that of the priesthood – rather than the expected sense of government or political authority.

Yes, you may have caught this intentional omission; it would be all too easy to lose sight of the profound power of Subsidiarity in a long debate on methods of government, so I defer that topic for the present. Or rather, in this book I explore the relevance of Subsidiarity to government by exploring its relevance to other systems, some more complex, some less. This example from my religion may be even more debatable than any topic relating to government, but I have intentionally chosen it because it is part of the Church's system which is *not* its government, and that is an important point to be demonstrated: Subsidiarity applies to systems even if there are other organizational aspects in the system, and provides benefits to each accordingly.

You will find something even more amazing about this example: it is one of the most *shallow* of the hierarchies I have mentioned, if not the most shallow. Many people, whether inside or outside the Church, are confused by the variety of offices or positions, sometimes from lack of knowledge of the terms or their application, sometimes because the same person may serve in more than one role. But in this particular example – the sacramental order, which is the true meaning of both the word *hierarchy* (sacred leadership) and the sacrament called *Holy Orders* – the order is actually no more than *four levels deep*. Indeed, few world-wide businesses, few governments, few organizations of any kind have only two layers intervening between the lowest order and the highest. The four layers are, from the lowest:

1. the laity – the common people who are not ordained. Ordinarily they are never ministers of sacraments, with the exception of Holy Matrimony (marriage), which the spouses administer to each other.

2. the priests – men ordained to the priesthood; they offer sacrifice (Holy Mass) and are the ordinary ministers of most sacraments, with the exception of Confirmation, Holy Orders (they cannot ordain new priests), and Matrimony (they bless and witness, but the spouses are the ministers).

3. the bishops – priests ordained to the episcopate; they administer Confirmation and ordain priests, but can only consecrate bishops when authorized.

4. the Pope – a bishop elected to "serve the servants"; in view of the order to Peter to "strengthen your brethren"[56] he is charged with the responsibility to appoint new bishops.

Among the many remarkable traits of this simple scheme is the result that every Catholic is joined to every other Catholic through no more than five other people: there is a parallel here in the circulatory system for nearly every cell of the body is at most only a very few cells away from a blood vessel – and therefore is always close to the heart, the principle of growth and the source of on-going life.

Here it is important to recall the upside-down character of this system: the higher orders exist for the sake of the lower ones. Just as an artery (of sufficient size) must have nourishment from arteries, each priest also needs a priest. He cannot absolve himself in Confession, nor anoint himself when sick. Nor can he make himself a priest. He must be called, just as the Apostles were called. The bishop is the superior of the priests according to the sacramental order: he makes new priests. The bishop needs priests, and even more importantly, needs the Pope, for he cannot make himself a bishop: he too must be called. Nor can a bishop make himself the Pope: there is a form of election and other rites by which he is also called to that service.

In each case of the non-lay members of the Church, there is the action of a special sacrament of service, wherein a man enters into a special role in the organization. That sacrament is called Holy Orders; it seems almost a pun, but indeed the *order* of the Church is *holy* and is nothing more than this action of service according to the rules of Subsidiarity as we have discussed.

Now for a surprise. I am not the first to describe it in this way.

In the introduction, I quoted St. Thomas Aquinas discussing the nature of order, where he indicates (much as I did) the arrangement of human affairs according to how one assists the other in accomplishment of a greater purpose. But his discussion, much like mine, serves a greater purpose; his is to set forth the technical details of Holy Orders:

A power directed to a principal effect naturally has lesser powers

---

[56] See Lk 22:32.

administering to it. ... Since then the power of Order [here meaning the sacrament] is directed chiefly to the consecration of Christ's body, and to its distribution to the faithful, and likewise to the cleansing of the faithful from their sins, there is need for a principal order, whose power extends chiefly to these things, and this is the Priesthood... [57]

Then Aquinas proceeds to the episcopal order, and to the office of Pope:

...the priest himself derives his power from the bishop: while all difficult matters regarding the faithful are reserved to bishops, by whose authority even the priests are able to do what they are appointed to do. Thus in his priestly actions, the priest uses things consecrated by a bishop; for instance in the celebration of the Eucharist, he uses chalice, altar and pall. Hence it is evident that the supreme power in the direction of the faithful belongs to the episcopal dignity. Now although the people are distributed among various dioceses and cities, nevertheless there is but one Church, and therefore only one Christian people. Consequently, just as a bishop is appointed as the head of a certain people and a particular Church, so must the whole Christian people be subject to one who is the head of the whole Church.

Again. The unity of the Church requires that all the faithful be of one faith. Now questions are wont to arise about matters of faith: and the Church would be divided by differences of opinion, unless its unity were safeguarded by the pronouncement of one. Therefore, in order to safeguard the unity of the Church, it is necessary that there be one who presides over the whole Church. [58]

Then, implicitly invoking the principle that "a thing is more perfect as it is more perfectly one," [59] Aquinas buttresses his argument by pointing out another reason for this hierarchical structure:

...the best form of government is when a people is governed by one: because the end of government is peace; since peace and unity of the subjects is the end of the governing authority: and unity is more fittingly ensured by one than by many. [60]

As I said, this particular example may be considered a debatable topic, though I would rather discuss it than the intricate details of governments far less old, far less wide-reaching, and far less stable than the Church. But one thing I do not think is arguable: such a structure is most certainly in keeping with the explicit directions of Jesus:

But Jesus called them to him and said: You know that the princes of the Gentiles lord it over them; and that they that are the greater, exercise power upon them. It shall not be so among you: but whosoever is the greater among you, let him be your minister. And

---

[57] Aquinas, *Summa Contra Gentiles* Book 4 Chapter 75
[58] Aquinas, *Summa Contra Gentiles* Book 4 Chapter 76.
[59] Kreyche, *First Philosophy*, 175.
[60] Aquinas, *Summa Contra Gentiles* Book 4 Chapter 76.

he that will be first among you shall be your servant. Even as the Son of man is not come to be ministered unto, but to minister and to give his life as a redemption for many. [61]

And in another place:

If then I being your Lord and Master, have washed your feet; you also ought to wash one another's feet. For I have given you an example, that as I have done to you, so you do also. Amen, amen, I say to you: The servant is not greater than his lord: neither is the apostle greater than he that sent him. If you know these things, you shall be blessed if you do them. [62]

Clearly there is an order in the supernatural structure of the Church, as St. Paul proposed with his "Analogy of the Body" which I considered previously. There is another, much less technical, but perhaps even more strong an example, found in Dante's *Paradiso*, which portrays the orderly, systematic structures of the Communion of Saints in its regular harmony: a system as regular and orderly as the motions of the planets, and having a most surprising Purpose, greatest of all possible Purposes: "The heavens shew forth the glory of God, and the firmament declareth the work of his hands. Day to day uttereth speech, and night to night sheweth knowledge." [63]

One final comment on this matter: it is not my purpose here to explore particular historical (or hypothetical) events; the Church knows far better the fallibility of her human components. But happily, as in the systems we have previously considered, even when those components fail, the good design of the Ecclesial system of Order maintains her pursuit of the Purpose.

---

[61] Mt 20:25-28
[62] Jn 13:14-17
[63] Ps 18(19):2-3

Part IV
Subsidiarity and Engineering

Jesus said: I am the vine: you the branches. He that abideth in me, and I in him, the same beareth much fruit: for without me you can do nothing.

Jn. 15:5

Chapter 1
Learning By Doing

If your aeroplane has a slight indisposition, a handy man may mend it. But, if it is seriously ill, it is all the more likely that some absent-minded old professor with wild white hair will have to be dragged out of a college or laboratory to analyze the evil. The more complicated the smash, the whiter-haired and more absent-minded will be the theorist who is needed to deal with it; and in some extreme cases, no one but the man (probably insane) who invented your flying-ship could possibly say what was the matter with it...
...if a thing is worth doing, it is worth doing badly.
GKC, *What's Wrong With the World*, CW4:43-4, 199

In Part II, we examined my scheme of file transport for cable TV local ad insertion. I must insist that this scheme is not a proposal, nor a suggestion, nor an abstract model, but indeed something that was actually accomplished, which did its work for almost exactly five and a half years: delivering about 200,000 spots which played over 200 million times, recording their performance in nearly 7 million spot-logs, providing a continuous display of the status of the machinery, reporting on problems, and all the rest. A few dozen people and about 200 computers, besides loads of additional equipment and other supporting personnel were part of the achievement. Certainly it would be misleading for me to suggest that Subsidiarity was applied to all portions of the effort, though once the term became commonplace at the company, and its power demonstrated, the principle began exerting its beneficial effect on other tasks beyond file transport.

But my work there was not in management: it was to design, implement, and maintain the ad insertion system. Like all real systems, our system required continual adjustment, augmentation and correction. I shall not go into all of the engineering aspects of the system, most of which are irrelevant to our purposes here, but there are some additional details which need to be specified: in particular, communication and failure, which are sufficiently important that I shall consider them in their own chapters. I will also provide a kind of extension from the technical into the human realm, by considering the role of certain human virtues in Subsidiarity.

I often wonder why there should be such a vast gap between the theoretical and the practical branches of subjects – indeed, a gap ringed as it

65

were with opposing forces who strive to widen the gap and rain destruction down on the other side – but all the while each side is continually sneaking across to steal the work accomplished by the other side. I wonder if anyone has ever read *The Consolation of Philosophy* by Boethius where he tells how the robe of Philosophy is adorned with the letters Theta (for theoretical) and Pi (for practical), or if anyone has noted how Hugh of St. Victor enumerated a list of "mechanical arts" as one of the four branches of philosophy. One scholar even notes[64] that Hugh uses the terms "arts" and "sciences" interchangeably! Moreover, as Chesterton noted[65] it is a principle of Scholastic Philosophy that we learn first from our senses, and a principle of modern Science that we learn by experiment – which is the same thing. Hence, to have even a simple system which exemplifies Subsidiarity (if only by analogy) provides us with a tool to discover more about this simple and important principle. The fact that portions of the system are mechanical actually help simplify our task, because we can examine things step by step without having to struggle with the issues of free will, of choice, of evil, of weakness and emotion and human personality and all the rest. We know that we are examining a "perfect" (though quite limited) design, but this means we can begin to understand the varieties of failure far more quickly. This is not a novel approach. The medical field begins with normal anatomy and physiology, even as it constantly notes the non-trivial variations – for it is almost impossible to study disease if we do not understand the natural being in the absence of disease. The same is done in various kinds of engineering, where "failure" (of, say, a bridge or aircraft) can be catastrophic.

There is another aspect of engineering to be considered – the simple idea of practicality. As part of his preparation for a major project, the engineer may write any number of technical papers about his task, but sooner or later he has to get up from his desk[66] and begin the real work of building.[67]

---

[64] Jerome Taylor notes that Chapter Three of Book Three of *The Didascalicon of Hugh of St. Victor* begins with this: "Chapter Three: Which Arts Are Principally to Be Read. Out of all the sciences named..." to which he adds this footnote: "40. That Hugh uses the terms 'art' and 'science' interchangeably is evident from a comparison of the title and opening sentence of this chapter." [pp. 86, 211]

[65] GKC: It might be called the appeal to Reason and the Authority of the Senses. GKC, *St. Thomas Aquinas*, CW2:429

[66] Admiral Morison noted this of many who write on the voyages of Columbus: "For no biographer of Columbus appears to have gone to sea in quest of light and truth. And you cannot write a story out of these fifteenth- and sixteenth-century narratives that means anything to a modern reader, merely by studying them in a library with the aid of maps. Such armchair navigation is both dull and futile." Samuel Eliot Morison, *Admiral of the Ocean Sea*, xvi. His masterly work was written after voyages in similar sailing ships upon the same waters and at the same times of year.

[67] As GKC observes: "Thus St. Thomas' work has a constructive quality absent from almost all cosmic systems after him. For he is already building a house, while the newer speculators are still at the stage of testing the rungs of a ladder, demonstrating the hopeless softness of the unbaked bricks, chemically analysing

In many cases of real-world activities, an engineer is not expected to give an exhaustive recounting of all the steps in his accomplishment, as if he were proving a theorem in geometry. He knows full well the laws of science, the spec sheets which describe the materials he uses, the cautions, the special cases, the side effects of one material in contact with another, and so forth. He knows the nature of the implementation, and can handle (or perhaps ignore) the risks of that particular implementation.

To take an instance from my own field, I may know full well that the formal complexity of a certain problem is intractable – in theory! But real software cannot be written while we tremble in fear of the "big O"![68] On the other hand, one ought not use up company resources trying to solve the Travelling Salesman Problem on 495 cities as I did before I knew anything about complexity theory.[69] This is akin to the famous quote from Chesterton about a fence,[70] or the dicta offered about Bach's use of parallel fifths: one must know the reason for the rule before one can have any hope of circumventing it. So now I proceed to write software anyway, because (for example) I may know from other considerations that the size of the problem is limited to what we call "small integers."[71] One must also know how to

---

the spirit in the spirit-level, and generally quarrelling about whether they can even make the tools that will make the house. Aquinas is whole intellectual aeons ahead of them, over and above the common chronological sense of saying a man is in advance of his age; he is ages in advance of our age. For he has thrown out a bridge across the abyss of the first doubt, and found reality beyond and begun to build on it." GKC, *St. Thomas Aquinas*, CW2:543.

[68] In computer science, "Big O" is the usual term which expresses the measure of the *complexity* of a problem: that is, how much time or resources such as working memory are required, depending on the mathematical "size" of the problem.

[69] Yes, this really happened, as funny as it sounds, and it really was for work, too, but it was long before the days when I wrote the software I've been describing. Complexity theory provides the definition of "Big O" and examines the inherent difficulty of various mathematical problems, such as the Travelling Salesman Problem. This is a famous difficult problem in computer science (the kind we call "NP complete"): A salesman must visit every one of a given number of cities. He starts and ends at the same place, and can visit them in any order. We want to find the *shortest* way of visiting all of them. This is by no means a purely theoretical or abstract puzzle, as the problem arises in a variety of real engineering situations, and hence demands a practical solution, if only one which is "good enough." However, the time required to find the true optimal solution grows as the factorial of the number of cities; as of 2012 it is unknown whether there can be a more efficient algorithm.

[70] As GKC observes: There exists in such a case a certain institution or law; let us say, for the sake of simplicity, a fence or gate erected across a road. The more modern type of reformer goes gaily up to it and says, "I don't see the use of this; let us clear it away." To which the more intelligent type of reformer will do well to answer: "If you don't see the use of it, I certainly won't let you clear it away. Go away and think. Then, when you can come back and tell me that you *do* see the use of it, I may allow you to destroy it." GKC *The Thing* CW3:157.

[71] "Small integers" means a severely limited scope of possible problems: it is

ignore such problems, by converting the problem into another form in which the intractable difficulties do not arise: these methods are sometimes called "engineering tricks" but in the real world, managers usually expect more of a result than an elegant and purely theoretical paper. They want to see an effective solution.[72]

There is no argument that the practical worker, especially an engineer, requires knowledge of the theory of his subject: "It is wrong to fiddle while Rome is burning; but it is quite right to study the theory of hydraulics while Rome is burning."[73] And the awareness of engineering tricks is useful to the scientist as well, for such things keep the real world before even the most theoretical scholar: they keep us humble, as they reveal the greater truths of reality.

---

perfectly practical to solve the Travelling Salesman Problem for 10 cities, which only requires examination of all 181440 possible paths. But for merely 18 cities there are about 180 trillion possible paths, which would be a challenge even for the supercomputers of 2012 to compute while one waited. For 495 cities the immense number of paths is $(494!)/2$, which starts with 4023790700 and is followed by another 1108 digits (roughly 4×10^{1117}) – a number far beyond any hope of direct solution, at least as our knowledge of complexity stands in 2012.

[72] Here is a striking example of subsidiarity at work: A co-worker once asked me to help when he found that his sophisticated calculator could not handle the computation of the factorial of ten thousand. A very simple revision of the problem by application of algebra easily reduced the problem to something he could handle.

[73] GKC, *What's Wrong With the World*, CW4:43

Chapter 2
The Secret of the Ad Insertion System

Every short story does truly begin with creation and end with a last judgment.

GKC, *The Everlasting Man*, CW2:379

The old fairy tale makes the hero a normal human boy; it is his adventures that are startling; they startle him because he is normal.

GKC, *Orthodoxy*, CW1:218

"The secret is," Father Brown said; and then stopped as if unable to go on. Then he began again and said: "You see, it was I who killed all those people."

GKC, "The Secret of Father Brown" in
The Secret of Father Brown

Since we are going to examine the ad insertion system in greater detail, I will have to reveal a secret about it – a secret that I kept from almost everyone while that system was running. Yes, like GKC's Father Brown, I have a secret to tell: you see, it was *I* who did all the work at that cable TV place I've been telling you about. I did the encoding, spot storage, spot transport, the playback and the monitoring. I cloned myself, by magic, and sent my duplicates out to work, both at Headquarters and in the Field – untiring, never eating or drinking or sleeping, I went to work in the dozens of places where...

It does sound like a fairy tale, doesn't it?

It would be all too easy to digress at this point – a very critical point, as you shall see – to talk about stories, and how I came to understand more about computer science by means of the Fairy Tale. (In fact, I wrote a novel-length story[74] about this company, just to try to explain more about it.) However, you will have to tolerate what will seem a brief digression here, because if you are to understand the nature of communication, and especially the topic of "Failure," you must first have a deeper understanding of "Purpose." And that means revealing some secrets, much as the author of a detective story reveals the truth.[75] It may come as a surprise to some, even in my own discipline; it may even be misunderstood. But I am not going to analyze this matter in detail: I merely need you to understand what I mean about my technique of developing computer systems such as the one I have

---

[74] That novel is called *Joe the Control Room Guy*.

[75] "Mystery stories are very popular, especially when sold at sixpence; but that is because the author of a mystery story reveals. He is enjoyed not because he creates mystery, but because he destroys mystery. Nobody would have the courage to publish a detective-story which left the problem exactly where it found it. That would rouse even the London public to revolution. No one dare publish a detective-story that did not detect." GKC ILN Aug 10 1907 in CW27:524

been telling you about.

There really isn't much to the secret. It just sounds a bit odd, and certainly not very technical, but that's because most computer scientists don't stop to think about what they are doing as they do it, or even sit back and review their method once they've finished doing it. But the entire nature of programming is nothing more than a very formal and precise way of writing instructions, much like cooking recipes or lab protocols or musical scores are written. The mere fact that *I myself* do not actually perform those instructions is irrelevant. Like any cook, any composer, I must know *exactly* what effect each of the ingredients or instruments will have at every stage – even if I am not eating the final food or hearing the final symphony.

Unlike food or music (except in some very special and limited cases[76]) computer programming must be able to deal with large variations in what is being manipulated, and even with the possibility of some disastrous problem arising. Composers as a rule do not put into their scores what to do if the E-string of the violin breaks during a solo – but software must handle such things, and arrange for a tidy retreat from the problem.

And so, in the work of designing our inserters, I actually *became* the inserter. Not in the simple sense of a child "becoming" an elephant, or like some wizard "morphing" into a cat. It is both more real, and also much less real than these. In doing the work of programming, one must remember the severe limits of the actual mechanical device one becomes: simple actions like storing a value in memory, retrieving it, adding and subtracting, comparing values and changing one's next step based on that comparison. Then there is another idea, far more powerful, but hard to describe, which we might call structural procedure hierarchy: the idea that one can build a mechanism to do something – for example, to compare two sequences of characters and decide which is alphabetically first – and then use that as if it were an elementary operation already part of the machine, like adding. This power of order and governance gives rise to "subroutines" under their various names, and other related but more mysterious powers like "threads" and "processes" which permit multiple tasks to be accomplished simultaneously. This may sound intricate, but many other professions do this all the time: a nurse may care for many patients at once; a chef making dinner often has several pots all cooking at once for the various courses.

Remember: I am not actually *doing* the work, in the headend, or at Headquarters – the machines will do that. But I must do it first, at least in some abstract sense, and then write the instructions for doing the work, or it will never be possible for the machines to do it at all.

We here touch the formal philosophy called *teleology*, or the study of purposes and of "ends" – that is "the reason why a thing is done." Since Subsidiarity, as applied to a given system, requires knowledge of the Purpose

---

[76] E.g. in cooking, the direction to "Bake until a straw inserted near the center comes out clean" or in music, the term "vamp until ready" given in the orchestral accompaniment to a stage production, or (as I once heard from my music director in high school) "take the second ending."

of that system (its "end," or goal) we need to grasp more fully the idea of Failure: that is, anything which interferes with the Purpose. Failure is when something goes wrong, so it is a major reason to appeal for assistance. Hence, we must first consider the role of communication within our example system: the ways in which direct as well as implicit appeals for help may be made.

Chapter 3
The Role of Communications in Subsidiarity

Quis Custodiet Ipsos Custodes?
(Who will watch the watchers themselves?)
Juvenal, Satire VI

...the object of my school is to show how many extraordinary things even a lazy and ordinary man may see if he can spur himself to the single activity of seeing.
GKC, Tremendous Trifles 6

"No machine can lie," said Father Brown, "nor can it tell the truth."
GKC, "The Mistake of the Machine"
in The Wisdom of Father Brown

The old joke that the Greek sects only differed about a single letter is about the lamest and most illogical joke in the world. An atheist and a theist only differ by a single letter; yet theologians are so subtle as to distinguish definitely between the two.
GKC, The New Jerusalem CW20:276

And a vision was shewed to Paul in the night, which was a man of Macedonia standing and beseeching him and saying: Pass over into Macedonia and help us.
Acts 16:9

Subsidiarity is about right order in society: the higher levels assisting the lower levels, yet not interfering with their own proper tasks. Assistance means that in some manner or other, the person being assisted somehow lacks something, and the person rendering assistance can supply that lack. True drama exists here – the drama of one who is generous but like the old widow in the Gospels, who gave of her want. (Mk. 12:42-44) There are also cases where the one who supplies does not diminish his own store – indeed, as Dante remarks intangible things can be given without diminution.[77] Such things may be left for poets and philosophers to consider, but there is an engineering aspect which we must examine if we wish to understand this matter of assistance: the matter of communication: How does the one needing help request it? What must be the nature of the request? What responsibilities are placed on the one asking, and on the one asked?

This topic will require further details of the technical nature of my system, but this detail is necessary if we wish to begin to grasp some of the far more complex issues within a purely human system. Clearly, in the general case, the informational needs at the various levels depend upon the precise character of the system, but we must also here remember the negative part of our definition, that the higher orders do not unduly interfere with the

---

[77] *Purgatorio*, Canto XV. Strangely, treating even this very difficult and human topic is quite easy in our example, because of the nature of electronic storage of information: an inserter can give copy after copy of a particular spot, and yet never diminish its own possession of that spot.

work of the lower. When we consider even a small, simple but fully human organization, it will be a challenge to specify the most suitable, most just, most respectful scheme of communication – so it will again be helpful for us to examine the requirements occurring in this example, the far simpler and mechanical system of ad insertion. For the purpose of our discussion, there are two forms of communication which occur among the various computers: file transport and the CUSTOS packet.

File Transport

All files within our system used a simple scheme, by which their names acted as a kind of combination tracking ticket and envelope: the file name consisted of (1) the name of the originating system, (2) the complete date and time of the file's generation, and (3) an indicator of the "type" of file – that is, the nature of its contents. There were a number of file types used in our system. Three were already mentioned in Part II as part of the actual implementation of Subsidiarity as applied to spot transport; the others were required by the nature of our Purpose, but also play a role in accomplishing Subsidiarity in a wider sense.

1. the Needed Spot Request files, or NSR, which a leaf produces in order to inform the portal of its needed spots.
2. the Portal Spot Request files, or PSR, which a portal produces in order to inform Headquarters of the spots needed within its subtree.
3. the spots themselves, which are also called MPEGs. These are sent from HOME to the portal, which sends them to the leaves.
4. The "schedule file" contains the instructions which tell the inserter when a spot is to play, and on what cable TV network. Each schedule is produced by Traffic depending on customer requests. A schedule is specific to the particular headend, and is sent from HOME to the portal, which distributes copies to its leaves.
5. The "spot-log" is the final product of the inserter: it contains the details of the actual work of spot playback done by the inserter. These spot-logs were sent from each leaf to its portal; the portal sent them to Headquarters, where they were accumulated. Eventually they were sent to Traffic, which produced the appropriate bills, or, in the case of failure to play, the missing plays were "made good" by an extension of the customer agreement.
6. The "complaint file" informs Headquarters of problems encountered by inserters in the Field (which is why they were called "complaints"). You may think of them as a simple form of e-mail produced by a program, as certain complaints were distributed by e-mail to the departments responsible for their resolution. They were also used for certain simple kinds of status reports.

You should note that each file type always flows in just one direction. The transport programs (FERRY on the inserters, and PUMP on HOME) were built to distinguish the correct types; if somehow an invalid type was found in the wrong place, it was moved to a holding area, and a "complaint file" was produced indicating that something unexpected had occurred. This elementary form of protection was anticipated in a famous dictum:

And which of you, if he ask his father bread, will he give him a stone? Or a fish, will he for a fish give him a serpent? Or if he shall ask an egg, will he reach him a scorpion? If you then, being evil, know how to give good gifts to your children, how much more will your Father from heaven give the good Spirit to them that ask him? [78]

The CUSTOS packet

This form of communication is kept distinct from file transport simply because the thing transported is not a file, but a small "chunk" of information. We might have chosen to use a file, but the information was of an ephemeral nature, valid only for a small time interval – these were being formed on the order of once a second, and there were easy ways of avoiding the clutter. Rather than go into technical details of network protocols, I shall merely suggest that this form of communication can be understood by analogy with "Twitter" – a popular way of keeping others apprised by reporting on one's activities in brief statements via the INTERNET. In order to keep Headquarters apprised of the current state of the nearly 200 inserters in the Field, we arranged the ENGINE to periodically report on the status of the inserter. This is nothing more than a fancy kind of heartbeat, which is produced every 150 seconds. The ENGINE collected the following information:

1. Name and network id of this inserter.
2. Date and time.
3. Current conditions of the machinery, including available disk space.
4. Several other status details not relevant to our discussion.

All this was reported in what we called a "CUSTOS packet." On a leaf, the ENGINE sent its packets to the portal responsible for that leaf. On the portal, the ENGINE received these packets from all the leaves of the subtree, and sent them, as well as its own packet, to HOME. Back at Headquarters, HOME sent these packets to each of the WATCHERs in the Control Room which could then display the current status of the machines out in the Field.

Now that we have considered *what* is being communicated, let us examine where these items come from and go to.

Communications at Level 1: between Leaf and Portal

A leaf inserter has only two links to the rest of the world. The first link may not be thought of as a communication element, but it is something more profound – and more obvious: the inserter is connected to the cable TV system, and when the inserter is working correctly, it plays out its

---

[78] Lk. 11:11-13

commercials (it "inserts" them) on the various cable networks it controls, and so its work becomes visible (its work is communicated) to the viewing public. This is really nothing more than a real-life instance of our Lord's words, "by their fruits you will know them."[79] Certainly many of our customers watched for their own commercials to play – if imperfections were noted in those spots, or (worse) if the spots failed to play when they were expected, our customers were quick to inform us. There was a big-screen television in our lunchroom where our own handiwork could be observed. This link may seem dull or trivially obvious, but in reality it is a critical form of communication: if no local spots play, there is something seriously wrong somewhere.

The second link is the "subtree network" which links the leaf to its portal. The subtree network provides the sole electronic (computer) connection to a leaf. As usual in such networks, this connection is bi-directional: the leaf can both send and receive, or both talk and listen. The ENGINE on the leaf uses the subtree network to send its CUSTOS packets to its portal. The transport program called "FERRY" on the leaf handles the delivery of files (such as NSRs and complaints) to the portal responsible for that leaf; it also dispatches any files which the portal sends to the leaf, putting spots in their proper place or passing schedules on to the ENGINE.

Communications at Level 2: between a Portal and HOME

In the case of a portal, there is an additional connection, which links the portal to the machinery at Headquarters – specifically the computer called HOME – by means of a satellite. In many ways, this satellite network link worked much like any hard-wired computer network, except for a severe limitation of speed, but we cannot go into the technical details here.[80] But the function of the link from a portal to HOME is very similar to the link from a leaf to its portal: in fact, it is this recursive or hierarchical structure which permits the strong analogy from the levels of machinery to the levels of the "rulers of thousands, hundreds, fifties, tens" recommended to Moses by Jethro. The communications between portal and HOME was parallel to that between leaf and portal: the ENGINE on the portal sent its CUSTOS packets (and those of its leaves) back to HOME. The FERRY sent files from the portal to HOME such as its PSR (Portal Spot Request), its spot-logs and its complaints, as well as any of these it received from its leaves; the portal also received files from HOME such as spots and schedules.

Summary of Communications Elements in the Field

It should now be clear that there are a number of strong parallels among the various components of this system:

---

[79] Mt 7:16

[80] Though I should note that it was this limitation of speed and other technical restrictions which demanded many of the special designs in the system I am describing.

1. At every headend, the portal is the parental communications hub for all the leaves of the subtree;

at Headquarters, HOME is the parental communications hub for all the portals of the Field.

2. A leaf requiring a spot indicates the need to its portal by sending it an NSR;

a portal requiring a spot indicates the need to HOME by sending it a PSR.

3. HOME sends a needed spot to a portal from its library;

a portal sends a needed spot to a leaf, either from itself or from another leaf in the subtree.

4. A leaf sends its status by a CUSTOS packet to its portal;

a portal sends its own status to HOME by a CUSTOS packet; it also sends all CUSTOS packets from its subtree.

In general, there is an "inbound" flow by which information travels from each leaf, through its portal to HOME. This path is used by spot request files (NSRs/PSRs), CUSTOS packets, spot-logs, and complaints.

There is also an "outbound" flow by which information travels from HOME to the portals, and then to its leaves. This path is used by schedules and spots (Mpegs).

What	Portal	Leaf	Why
spot request file	PSR out (to HOME)	NSR out (to portal)	requests spots
spot file	in (from HOME)	in (from portal)	supplies spots
CUSTOS packet	out (to HOME)	out (to portal)	gives current status
schedule file	in (from HOME)	in (from portal)	when to play spots
spot-log file	out (to HOME)	out (to portal)	reports what was done
complaint file	out (to HOME)	out (to portal)	reports info/emergency

Communications at Level 3: between HOME and the Control Room

This level is significantly more interesting than the others, since it is hybrid: it is the link between the mechanical side and the human side. However, we are not here considering the very interesting issues of physiology or attention spans, or the design of human interfaces; we are simply examining the major kinds of information which our machinery presented to the Control Room operators. Rather than distracting you with the technical details as presented by WATCHER (our monitoring program) I will describe the various kinds of information which was presented. In the Control Room, WATCHER was continuously displayed on four huge theater-style screens, providing a visual report of the status of the Field even to visitors out in the hallway. In order to provide the maximum assistance to the operators in their work, WATCHER could present a variety of different views[81] , but I will only mention those which directly assist us in our study.

From our studies in Part II, it should be clear that the primary "request

---

[81] I should mention that some of these were specifically requested by the operators; in this case, Subsidiarity was being enacted at the strictly human level.

for assistance" at this level of the system occurs when a spot is not present in the MASTER LIBRARY. This request requires the operator to *encode* that needed spot – that is, convert the spot which Traffic supplies as a physical tape into an equivalent electronic form called MPEG. The final step performed by the operator causes that spot (in its MPEG form) to be entered into the MASTER LIBRARY. These "spot lists" were indeed displayed by WATCHER. However, in the wider sense of Subsidiarity – any appeal for assistance from the Field – there are a number of additional actions which humans had to perform in order to supply that assistance. These were actions which no machine can perform, and so they required human intervention. Since a machine cannot always "ask" for what it needs (especially if it has failed, for example) there must be a variety of signals which clue in the operators about the status of the machinery: these are grouped as "headend status" and "complaints."

Spot Lists

WATCHER provided a display of the current spot transport activity as reported by PUMP. This could be presented as either of two lists:

1. The "To Be Sent" list is the summary of all spots which were to be delivered to the Field. This gave us awareness of the work of HOME in satisfying the requests of the various PSRs from the Field. The importance of this list will be noted in our chapter on Failure.

2. The "To Be Encoded" list is the summary of all spots which were being called for, but not yet available in the MASTER LIBRARY. As we noted in Part II, this display constitutes the "appeal" for assistance from the machinery at Headquarters to the operators. The operators used this list to arrange their work of encoding. As mentioned earlier, the final step in the process of encoding was a mechanical "notification" to PUMP that a spot had been added; the spot was then scheduled for transport and so it was removed from the "To Be Encoded" list and appeared on the "To Be Sent" list.

Headend Status

WATCHER provided a display of "telltales" – a computerized form of the classic red and green indicator lamps[82] used in all sorts of equipment control boards. This was simply a list of all the headends of the Field, together with a colored region, usually a small green circle. The color (and sometimes the shape) indicated the "health" of that headend. There were arrangements which permitted the operators to see additional details about the various inserters comprising that headend.

1. The continuing arrival of CUSTOS packets indicated that the various inserters were still "alive" – that is up and running, and functioning correctly.

---

[82] GKC: "The word 'signal-box' is unpoetical. But the thing signal-box is not unpoetical; it is a place where men, in an agony of vigilance, light blood-red and sea-green fires to keep other men from death." GKC, *Heretics* CW1:55. Note that GKC knew the "signal-box" from its use on railroads, but in our automotive age we may also understand it as a traffic light.

The machinery provided a certain "grace period" but if no signals arrived, the inserter was assumed to have a problem, and the telltale went red. Other mechanical issues were also indicated this way. Since the portal was the single communications link between its leaves and HOME, if it failed, its leaves appeared to "fail" as well, even if they were still functioning.

2. These packets contained information about the current resources – most importantly, how much remaining free space was available on their disk drives. If the free space sank below a certain minimum, a problem was signalled.

3. The arrival of spot-logs also indicated proper functioning; moreover, since these were most critical for the sake of the ultimate performance of our company, we kept a close watch that these were properly delivered. The spot-log delivery gave a secondary indication, since their ongoing delivery indicated that the file transport machinery was healthy.

4. There were a number of other technical details indicating the status of the machinery which helped the operator determine where to look or what to do about the situation. For example, the inserter had eight playback cards which did the actual insertion of the spots, and the status of each playback card was reported in the packet. If one card failed, the operator could request Field Services to replace that single card. (We must here note another instance of Subsidiarity: as monitoring had to be maintained 24/7, the operators could only perform whatever was possible from within the Control Room, either by network or other means. If the problem in the Field required on-site repair, Operations had to appeal to Field Services for assistance, and a Field Tech would then drive out to that location to do the work.)

Complaints

The primordial design of a complaint was simply a means for a program (whether running on a computer in the Field or in Headquarters) to announce that it had detected a serious problem. A complaint registered on one of the monitoring screens in the Control Room, and had the appearance of an e-mail, indicating what computer it came from, the date and time, and other such information, including the severity of the situation, and any additional details which were known. They were so useful that we added several "informative" kinds of complaints, one of which is the "Daily Log." Every day, just after midnight, the ENGINE on every inserter would perform its "daily chores" which produced a detailed report of the inserter status. This report was placed into a complaint file, which was sent back to Headquarters and archived, to provide us with information for trouble-shooting.

Communications Among Higher Levels

Beginning with Operations, all the higher levels of the system were human, and used the usual human communications protocols, adapted to business common practices: the spoken word (including voice-mail), written notes and memos and documents, and e-mails. I might emphasize that certain aspects of the departmental organization underscored the "negative" dimension of Subsidiarity (the higher levels must not interfere unduly with the work of the lower levels), some of which I might mention here:

1. The Traffic Department personnel were permitted to come into the Control Room in order to deliver the physical tapes containing the spots to be encoded, or to retrieve them. They had some awareness of what was displayed on WATCHER, but were not expected to perform monitoring. They were not permitted contact with the machinery. Only Operations and Traffic (and on occasion Field Services) were permitted into the Control Room.

2. The Operators could use certain forms of electronic "remote access" to adjust or repair machinery in the Field, but could not actually travel out to the headends to work on the machinery directly. This could only be done by members of Field Services, which was the only department of our company who entered the actual headends.

3. Operations could only perform certain common tasks, or high-level corrective steps on any computer, whether in Headquarters or out in the Field. Direct manipulation of specific files was forbidden. More severe mechanical problems required the Operators to appeal to higher-level specialists such as the Tech Shop (for hardware support) or Development (for software support), which also maintained their own cooperative segregation of effort.

4. The Operators were not permitted to produce or alter the schedules (the instructions to the inserters), nor the spot-logs (the records of work performed by the inserters), though they acted as gate-keepers at the frontier between Traffic and the file transport machinery. The files and their contents were solely in charge of Traffic.

5. Ad Sales personnel had direct contact only with Traffic and with the Customers. Generally neither Ad Sales nor Customers ever entered any of the other departments, though all visitors were always shown the Control Room – there was a huge glass wall so visitors could admire the colors[83] on its four big monitoring screens.

---

[83] Visitors also puzzled over the Latin quotes on WATCHER, and the ever-shifting eyes of CUSTOS. But these details are beyond the scope of our text.

Chapter 4
Subsidiarity and Failure

Father, I have sinned against heaven and before thee, I am not now
worthy to be called thy son.

Lk. 15:21

It is always simple to fall; there are an infinity of angles at which
one falls, only one at which one stands.

GKC, *Orthodoxy* CW1:306

The following might sound like fiction, but it really happened (and more
than once, too!) I was asleep, in bed, at my home... and then I heard:

Beep, beep. "Hey Doc you there?"

My eyes popped open. *Oh, great. Something's wrong.* I rolled over and
grabbed the phone, glancing at my clock: 02:35 AM. I pushed the transmit
button. "Yeah. What's up, Joe?"

That, of course, is literal Subsidiarity in action: the appeal for assistance.
A bit awkward, but necessary. There are many such roles in society: police,
physicians and nurses, priests, utility workers, certain government officials –
and parents – all have to be "on-call," available to their subordinates 24/7, all
day, all night, every day throughout the year. It would be helpful to study this
aspect of the responsibility and the accruing dignity, the formal and practical
relations between those who serve and those who are served – and perhaps
someday that study will be written.

But I have another reason for recounting the story of how the night shift
occasionally had to wake me in the dead of night. For they called me when
there was something seriously wrong with one of the machines of our system
– a problem which (like the judges Moses set over tens and fifties) was
beyond their abilities to resolve.

This matter of failure within a system relying upon Subsidiarity is an
important one. It was raised by a comment from an insightful student, and is
by no means an easy one, though a lawyer or a theologian or logician may
have a glib response. But a careful Scholastic will ask questions about this
issue, revealing the true complexity. What *is* wrong? What is the nature of
the failure? What is its cause? What is its effect? What remedy is there to
solve the issue at hand? And, perhaps the most subtle of all: What action can
be taken to deal with similar cases in the future?

Ah. At first this will sound like a grad student gearing up for a nice long
dissertation. But these thoughts and more flew through my own mind as I
spoke with the Control Room operator, for these are the great questions all
such support personnel must ask. It is part of the method of *diagnosis* and the
subsequent step of corrective action.

What do we mean when we say "failure" in a system? Simply, it is whenever the Purpose of that system is not being attained. That is, one of the rules of that system is being broken. The variety of failures therefore depends on the specific character of the system, and this makes the study very difficult, if we are to get anywhere without making such broad generalizations that the results are mere platitudes. Let us, then, take our spot-transport ad insertion system example, and see what we may learn from the wide variety of failures we actually encountered, either during development or during the 5.5 years the system was functioning. We must recall the limitations of the analogy from our system to human organizations, since our system is partially mechanical – but as we proceed, we shall find that this will work to our advantage. The formal issue that the machines did not "choose" to fail does not enter discussion; we are not talking about guilt.

We must also add another question to our earlier list, assuming the Scholastic we consult knows computer science: *How do we know about such failures in the first place?* That is, how do we arrange things so we'll find out "up front" when something goes wrong, instead of when it's too late? That is, how do failures make themselves known, and if they do not, or cannot, how do we actually monitor the status of the system? The study of Failure helps illuminate certain necessary qualities of the required communication scheme: in particular, the idea of having a secondary or associated communication path which I shall call "awareness" rather than "monitoring," which has some unpleasant implications as applied to human situations. Our system also suggested another idea which is not obvious: that the higher levels can acquire certain kinds of information about the work of lower levels: that is, they may obtain some awareness about them by a variety of indirect or secondary means, not necessarily by the ordinary or principal path. (By analogy from anatomy, we came to call this idea "anastomosis," referring to the arrangement of alternate paths within the circulatory system.)

The Rules

What are these "rules" we speak of? There are three sets of rules which govern a system based upon Subsidiarity.

1. The metarules of Subsidiarity.
2. The rules which govern the system under discussion (the "rules of the game").
3. The laws which underlie the system: Physical, Natural, Moral, Legal, Social.

The highest is the metarules of Subsidiarity, which do not change the system (the Order, Purpose, Abilities, and Limitations of the system) but modify the Order and the lines of communication to produce a more efficient (that is, productive or effective) system. The second set of rules are those which govern the particular system itself: we might call them the "rules of the game" as if the system we consider is a sports team. They are not properly rules of Subsidiarity, but those of the system: the company, the club, the nation, or other organization. The third, and deepest set of "rules" are those laws which underlie the system, including those called Physical, Natural, Moral, Legal, and Social.

In order to speak about failure, we need to consider what kind of rule is being broken. The examples which follow are mostly from the mechanical portion of our system, but they are sufficiently simple as to readily suggest analogies in a comparable human situation – we must keep in mind the fact that while a human can (for a short time) act like a computer, no computer can ever act like a human.

The Metarules of Subsidiarity

The metarules of Subsidiarity are the transcendent ideas which speak of how the various members of a given organization (or system) are to interact. They are found in both negative and positive forms in the Papal encyclicals we have already studied: the "higher" members must not transgress on the "lower," but rather must supply assistance as may be necessary. Implied by this ordering, an additional rule is imposed, which we might call the "rule of the hierarchy" which requires the higher layers to maintain a degree of awareness for the layers lower than them.

This layered view is of the essence of Subsidiarity, and so I insist on this "layered" sense, using the terms "metarule" and "transcendent" because Subsidiarity imposes a "higher" order upon the Order which is part of that system, and adds duties and responsibilities, all of which center on the right use of communication within that system.

As we mentioned previously, Subsidiarity is *the* way of doing things in any complex system, and to the extent it is used, that system is more effective. So, if the "rules" of Subsidiarity are *not* followed, that system is merely deprived of being effective. Things will continue to work, but often to futility, to frustration, to disappointment, and (if carried to extremes) to failure of the Purpose of that system.

In the abstract, a human organization founded upon Subsidiarity might therefore fail the metarules in several ways:

Metarule 1 is the positive rule, "higher supports lower in case of need." There are several forms of its failure:

1.a When a higher member refuses to assist upon the appeal of a lower member.

1.b When a lower member fails to appeal when aid is required.

1.c When a lower member nullifies the properly rendered assistance of the higher member.

1.d When a lower member requests aid from an inappropriate superior. ("Sheila's Case 1")

1.e When a lower member requests aid for something it already can perform for itself. ("Sheila's Case 2")

Metarule 2 is the negative rule, "higher must not arrogate functions of lower." Its violation is simply stated:

2. When a higher member interferes with the work of a lower member.

Metarule 3 is implied by the hierarchical structure, since Subsidiarity is *complete* – that is, both the positive and negative rules apply in a complete sense to all parts and levels of the system. Recall that we always consider that there are *three* (or more) levels, and not merely two. Thus, levels higher than the two which are in the "appealer/appealed-to" situation must themselves be concerned with the health of the system, and oversee that there is due regard for the two rules of Subsidiarity. Since there are two rules to be obeyed, there can be two ways in which this metarule is broken:

3.a When the positive rule is broken: that is, when a third-level member fails to correct the second-level member who fails to respond to an appeal from the first-level member for assistance.

3.b When the negative rule is broken: that is, when a third-level member fails to correct the interference of a second-level member with the work of a first-level member.

Note: I have used the terms *third*, *second*, and *first* to indicate the relative nature of the levels involved. In a real example, there can be any number of levels. The first level, of course, is the lowest, the one that actually does the work of the system. (In our example, the first level is the leaf inserters, but we must keep in mind that a portal is also an inserter.)

The Rules of the System

These rules are specific to the given system under consideration. They depend on the nature of the Purpose of the system and its implicit order (that is, the order which the system would have even if Subsidiarity was not part of it), but I suggest here that these rules are considered separate from the underlying laws imposed on all humans. After all, the laws of physics or of morality do not give specific details on how jobs are performed, how games are played, how clubs are organized: "The truth is, of course, that the curtness of the Commandments is an evidence, not of the gloom and narrowness of a religion, but, on the contrary, of its liberality and humanity. It is shorter to state the things forbidden than the things permitted; precisely because most things are permitted, and only a few things are forbidden."[84]

The complexity of dealing with this ambiguity gives us one of the strongest arguments for our use of a very specific and limited example. Our cable TV example has a very simple rule: "Play the commercials provided by our customers, in the regions, on the networks, according to the repetitions and at the dates and times they have requested – as far as that may be possible given the limitations imposed on our system."

These limitations are not those in what I have been calling Limitations as they relate to Subsidiarity, but those imposed, as it were, by nature, by the

---

[84] GKC, ILN Jan 3 1920 CW32:18

"game" of cable television, by the concept of ad insertion, and so forth. These limitations cannot be alleviated by "appeals for assistance" within the system as we have it.[85] For example:

1. Any given cable television network only permits local ad insertion at certain stated times and at certain stated intervals of time. The most common arrangement was a 120-second commercial "break" which occurred at times of the form xx:28 and xx:58 – that is, about two minutes before the half-hour, and two minutes before the hour. Since a typical spot is 30 seconds long, one "break" could accommodate four spots. There were a total of 48 such "breaks" in one day, which means that no more than 192 commercials could be scheduled in one day for one particular network. This is a "rule of the game" and not subject to "appeal" in the sense that change *within our system* could be accomplished. A violation of this rule was comparable to a team having too many men on the field in a football game, and penalties could be imposed.

2. The regions in which a customer might request his spot to be inserted were dependent on the arrangements of the actual distribution of the signals made by the cable television suppliers. For example, in our system, the huge suburbs of Philadelphia were divided among a number of headends; Harrisburg, the state capital, is split by the Susquehanna River, and was supplied by two headends; a small town like Reading is supplied by only one headend. Because ad insertion in our system was at the headend level, it was not possible to arrange a finer division of the viewing public than that.[86]

3. As you might expect, we had more than one customer who wanted spots to be aired. It was the task of Traffic (working together with the Ad Sales team) to arrange things so that the most customers would be satisfied. Presumably the use of a pricing scale helped manage the demand for the choice "breaks" (such as those during "prime time") and the lesser ones during the small hours of the night.

The Underlying Laws

The underlying laws are those which apply in general to all humans, regardless of their particular organization into the system under consideration. I use the word *law* in a broad sense, to comprise all dictates and prohibitions from whatever source, whether Physical, Natural, Moral, Civic (be they national or local), or Social (including tradition or custom).

Since the application of these bodies of law to the system under discussion depend on that system, it is hard to speak in general. However, we will consider some examples which may help.

---

[85] Though it is of course possible for "our system" to appeal to *another* system – that is, perhaps to request assistance from a particular cable television network, from suppliers, from a branch of government or so forth. See the following chapter on the extension of Subsidiarity.

[86] In 2012, the situation is different, with the use of set-top boxes and digital machinery, but that system would be a different kind of game, and have different rules.

1. The content of certain spots was controlled according to laws governing propriety: so-called *adult* material could not be inserted on a children's network. This was normally regulated by Traffic.

2. Certain spots were "dated" – that is, were not to be played after a certain date: for example, a statement from a candidate running for political office, or an ad for a special holiday sale. This was normally regulated by Traffic.

3. Exterior failures of various kinds which compelled us to refrain from playing spots. The classic example of this occurred on September 11, 2001, when nearly every cable TV network "went live" with coverage of the tragedy. Our records showed that roughly 30 percent of our spots failed to play – the worst performance recorded for any single day in the 5.5 years our system was in use.

4. The "fat-fingering" error: an average of 100 spots a day were encoded, and several thousand were scheduled. Despite careful attention to detail and cross-checking, typing errors were made, resulting in a non-existent spot, or an incorrect reference to an existing spot.

5. The tape as supplied by the customer might be "bad" – either poorly recorded, or corrupt in some way, so that it could not be encoded. When such cases were encountered by Operations the tape was returned to Traffic, and thence to the customer.

6. With somewhere around 600 disk drives in continuous heavy use, any imperfection was bound to show up eventually. To be specific, every so often a spot was stored on the disk drive at an area where the magnetic surface was poor. No problem was noted when the spot was placed there, but later, when the spot had to be played, the information was garbled as it was read from the disk.[87] This defect might not be noted by the software which read the disk, but the garbled information would render the spot "corrupt": when the corrupt part was sent to the playback machinery, the playback of that spot would fail.

Examples of Metarule Failure

1. Violation of the positive rule:
1.a. When a higher member refuses to assist upon the appeal of a lower member

This error occurred during development of the spot transport system, as I formulated the precise definition of the "NSR" or Needed Spots Request

---

[87] Imagine that you are photocopying the page of an old book, and the edge of the page crumbles – a fragment falls onto the copier as you put the book down on the glass. The copy now has a "corrupt" letter or word. You can further imagine that the book is a cookbook in some language you cannot read, and you are making a copy for a cook who *can* read that language. You may be in for a very unpleasant surprise at dinner.

file transmitted from the leaf to the portal. At one point, the NSR "generator" had been adjusted, but the corresponding "acceptor" was not adjusted in the same way, so the portal could not "hear" what the leaf "requested."

How did we find out? WATCHER reported no spots needed at that headend, but spots were not playing. Since the leaf was deprived of the spots it needed, it would report "cannot play due to missing spot." However, the portal (which is responsible for the needs of the subtree of that headend) indicates that all its needs were satisfied.

Since this is a mechanical system, the correction requires action by the designer. But, by analogy, we can consider the "refusal" of the appeal to be *willful*, whether polite or impolite, malevolent or otherwise. (Note that we have already dealt with the case where the one appealed to cannot *directly* or *immediately* supply the need; that is the whole essence of Subsidiarity.)

Why is this interesting? In a real human organization, an individual frustrated with a direct request to his superior can usually appeal to a higher layer: "I'd like to speak to your manager, please." This important quality of Subsidiarity is actually enshrined in the First Amendment to the American Constitution, which guarantees the right "to petition the government for redress of grievances"; it also appears in Canon Law, specifically Canon 212 §§ 2 and 3, and Canon 213.

However in our example, it is impossible for the leaf to *appeal for its needed spots* to HOME or any higher order. There are two additional channels which lead from every leaf, through the portal, to higher orders.[88] (1) The "real-time" status of all leaves is reported to the Control Room monitors. (2) The daily performance of every inserter is reported by its spot-logs which are returned to Traffic. So if a leaf is unduly deprived of its needs, while the portal may be "unaware" of that deprivation, the higher orders are informed of the situation.

Hence, we see that a degree of *awareness* of the work of lower layers is required by higher layers, if they are to protect the Purpose, and avoid this form of failure.

1. Violation of the positive rule:
1.b When a lower member fails to appeal when aid is required.

In our system, this case is all but identical to the previous one, differing only in the exact location of the badly-written portion of the software. But then a failure to appeal for aid has the same effect on the Purpose as a failure to supply aid when requested: in both cases, the need is not satisfied, and it falls to the higher orders to handle the matter.

We might here indicate that in the human situation, this case might arise

---

[88] We note here an analogy to certain aspects of alternative paths within the human body (e.g. the vagus nerve, or the circulatory system) as considered in part III.

when a person is too proud to know when to ask for help, or when some difficulty exists between the lower individual and his direct superior, or so forth.

1. Violation of the positive rule:
    1.c When a lower member nullifies the properly rendered assistance of the higher member.

This case never occurred in my recollection, but I can construct an approximate example. Let us imagine that at a certain time, a leaf requires very many spots, and its disk drive is nearly full. Now, a new schedule comes in, requiring one additional spot. The leaf appeals to the portal, and begins to receive it. However, that one additional spot will not fit, so the transport fails. But the request remains outstanding, so the portal will try again, and again... Since that needed spot never actually arrives, it cannot play – and so the same situation applies as above. Note, however, that the Control Room will receive a warning about the nearly full disk, which must be dealt with by other means.

In the human case, this might be due to greed – for example, when the request is based on a lie, and the aid is used for selfish purposes, and not to the Purpose – or through some form of incompetence or other weakness of the requestor.

1. Violation of the positive rule:
    1.d When a lower member requests aid from an inappropriate superior. ("Sheila's Case 1")

In our example, a leaf cannot make a direct appeal to another leaf for a needed spot. In fact, the leaf knows *nothing* about the other members of its sub-tree, except for its portal. This, of course, is by design, but we can infer the difficulties which would arise from a sloppy or ill-considered networking scheme. (This, in fact, had been the case before we installed our system.) For example, one of the difficulties which arise from permitting each leaf to "do its own thing" would be that multiple spot transports could occur simultaneously. This causes a serious degradation of all transports, since there are hidden costs (of overhead and network contention) associated with such ungoverned network use. Hence, good design is necessary, which in the human example carries the implication that good reason – common sense and courtesy – be used. One does not call a dentist when one's sewer is clogged.

1. Violation of the positive rule:
    1.e When a lower member requests aid for something it already can perform for itself. ("Sheila's Case 2")

This is the classic case of "asking someone else to do something one can do for himself" and which therefore ought not require any appealing to others. However, despite a certain attitude of exalting "self-esteem" which is all too prevalent in some areas today, there is another attitude by which one is expected to submerge one's personal independence and authority in matters of personal importance. This leads to the expectation that we ought to be able to have "specialists" who will handle every conceivable task for us. But that is not right:

> The democratic contention is that government (helping to rule the tribe) is a thing like falling in love, and not a thing like dropping into poetry. It is not something analogous to playing the church organ, painting on vellum, discovering the North Pole (that insidious habit), looping the loop, being Astronomer Royal, and so on. For these things we do not wish a man to do at all unless he does them well. It is, on the contrary, a thing analogous to writing one's own love-letters or blowing one's own nose. These things we want a man to do for himself, even if he does them badly.[89]

As you can see, the issue rapidly becomes nearly unmanageable when left to the strictly human case. Is this something a man should do for himself, or is it something perhaps requiring a specialist to accomplish? Fortunately, we find the answer readily by analogy from our cable TV example, and I seem to recall the precise case as having occurred during testing, if not during the actual life of the system. Let us presume that a certain leaf has a particular spot, which it requires, but, due to some flaw in the work of FERRY, the NSR for the leaf still shows that spot as needed! Hence, the portal will again command the transport of that spot to the leaf, and this will occur over and over again, until someone notices that things are running poorly within that subtree. The problem arising from this flaw is one of lowered efficiency, and of wrongful interference in the ordinary work of the system. The portal is doing work it ought not be required to do. In the more general case, demanding assistance from a superior in one's own work will unduly tax the resources of that superior, and lessen his effectiveness, or perhaps take him away from those who truly need assistance.

2. Violation of the negative rule:
2.a When a higher member interferes with the work of a lower member.

This very interesting case actually occurred in our system. Here a few examples:

Example 1. During certain maintenance tasks, an operator sets a network "into test," but then neglects to clear this when the maintenance is completed. When a network is put "into test" the inserter is prevented from playing any spots. Moreover, the viewing public will most likely not be receiving that TV network: either they see static, or black, or a test signal.

---

[89] GKC *Orthodoxy* CW1:250

This "test" state shows up on WATCHER with a special warning signal[90] which the operators knew meant serious trouble, since it would be far worse if the viewing public complains to the cable company about it.

Very instructive. One might comment on how this suggests the "public" effects of private sins, but that will go too far from our topic. Obviously, if the "test" mode persisted very long, many spots would not play, and this would be duly reported in the spot-logs, so Traffic would learn eventually, but it would no doubt be detected long before that. Clearly, this again points to the need for variant forms of communication – the provision of a larger awareness of the system's activity, especially to the higher levels of its members. (Clearly, Subsidiarity answers "Yes" to Cain's question, "Am I my brother's keeper?"[91])

Example 2. When an inserter failed completely (e.g. its system disk was corrupted), then a new leaf had to be installed. At the moment when the new leaf is connected, it has no spots at all in its disk drive – and then it is given all its schedules, and the full complement of scheduled spots are required.

I mention this extreme case because it occurred with some regularity (These machines do fail for various reasons; we shall see more of this form of failure in a little while.) But, though there was inescapable (indeed, required) interference from a higher order in the work of a lower, this case was one of the chief demonstrations of the power of Subsidiarity. For no sooner did that new inserter begin to work than a large NSR went to the portal, which began to supply its needs. (As this is *local* ad insertion, any spot which plays on one leaf will often play on other leafs of that subtree.) In fact, a fresh, completely empty inserter was often playing spots within minutes of its being installed and going live. Meanwhile, a new PSR went back to HOME, and PUMP was busy sending out the spots which were specific to that leaf. It was this particular surge in spot transport that made "subsidiarity" a common word in the Control Room, as it was the expected activity when a new inserter went live.[92]

Example 3. This one might actually be called "interference by an outsider" rather than by a superior. Every so often we noted a certain portal failing to send back its status, and it was unable to receive any spot or send back its PSR or other files. We checked and found it to be running correctly, but the satellite link was failing. This happened almost regularly during the work week, but not on nights or weekends, so we suspected some kind of human activity, due to certain industries in that area. But it made for difficulties at times, so we sent technicians out to the site. In a rather dramatic piece of detection, it was learned that someone was sitting in a truck

---

[90] It was a black pentagonal "home plate" symbol, suggesting a skull.
[91] Gen. 4:9.
[92] Yes, you could actually see this happening. It was impressive to WATCH.

nearby – and his truck had an active radar detector! When that detector was turned on, our signal dropped; when it was turned off, the signal was restored.

3. Failure of the hierarchy

3.a When the positive rule is broken: that is, when a third-level member fails to correct the second-level member who fails to respond to an appeal from the first-level member for assistance.

This case occurred when the network link between a leaf and its portal was broken after the leaf had sent an NSR requesting a certain spot which was not in the subtree. The portal sends a PSR to HOME, which sends the spot to the portal. The PSR now changes, since the portal "knows" it has the spot it needs, so HOME thinks everything is fine at that headend. But in reality the poor leaf is still missing the spot, since the portal cannot send the spot down to the leaf! Remember, HOME is not being inattentive or uncaring; it is a machine and has not been designed to handle such a situation. But the system will note an anomaly and report it to the human portion which can respond: as we have seen in our discussion on communication, such a severing of communications breaks the on-going heartbeats (the CUSTOS packets) which keep the headend telltale in WATCHER green. Once the telltale goes red, Operations will notice the problem and respond to the situation. (In this case, Operations would have to appeal to Field Services to drive to the headend and replace the network link.)

3.b When the negative rule is broken: that is, when a third-level member fails to correct the interference of a second-level member with the work of a first-level member.

We might consider the case when the portal of a headend has failed completely. The leaves of the headend depend on the portal for their spots and for other things. However, except when HOME has a spot to be sent to that portal, HOME does not "know" anything about the portal, and as it is a machine, it cannot deal with the failure of the portal. As in the above example, such a severe failure is readily reported by WATCHER, and Operations will investigate, most likely appealing to Field Services to take a replacement portal to the headend.

Errors in Communication

As Chesterton's Father Brown noted, "no machine can lie, nor can it tell the truth." At the same time, there are a variety of things which can go wrong even in mechanical forms of communication – yes, even when machines communicate with each other. The topic is far too large to attempt to summarize here, but a very large amount of the hidden work of computers is devoted to the attempt to reduce the chance of error as far as possible: there are entire branches of mathematics (e.g. Galois Field Theory) devoted to the techniques of error detection and correction. Most people who deal with electronic forms of communication talk about its wonders, but "Can you hear me now?" has become a common joke among users of cell-phones, and those who use the INTERNET often gripe about its speed, not realizing that speed is the primary sacrifice made to maintain accuracy. For example, one simple error-correcting scheme is to repeat the message three times. I could digress here to a consideration of the mysticism of "three,"[93] but there is no mysticism to this well-known and mathematically sound approach – we used it ourselves for certain tasks.

We also used another simple concept from networking standards, the embedding of messages within standard "packaging." This sounds complex but is a simple idea. For example consider how payroll might work in a large company. Each check is put into its own envelope. Then, all envelopes for a given department are put into a large "transport" envelope, which is addressed to the supervisor of that department. This technique is even used within the living cells: certain messenger RNA sequences are generated with a "poly-A tail" which indicates that they are to be delivered to another location within the cell.[94] We used something similar in our system. I cannot go into all the technical details of this technique, but I must say that every one of the half-billion packets sent over our satellite began with the mystical bit pattern 01000001 01101101 01000100 01100111, which is the ASCII code for "AmDg," the initials of the Ignatian motto *Ad majorem Dei gloriam*. Any message received which did not start with this pattern was rejected.[95] Though it may sound merely poetic, the underlying meaning here is that each message within the system must be consistent with the "whole message" – that is, with the Purpose of the system.

There is one further point I must make about communication – it is a fact well-known to humanity, but it is proclaimed more dramatically when we are forced into the consideration of technical details by trying to apply our ideas of "talking and listening" to machines. To put it simply, communication requires a two-way path. When two people are conversing, there are numerous, almost unnoticed forms of "feedback" by which the speaker maintains an awareness that his words are being received by the listener. The point might be readily understood from the technique used in police forces and radio dispatchers: received information is repeated back to

---

[93] The reality of *three* spans everything from the Trinity to the Watson-Crick code which maps DNA nucleotide triplets into amino acids, to the three-consonant roots of Semitic words. But the repeat must be odd, and three is merely the smallest odd number of repeats. Indeed the reliability improves with a larger number of repetitions, though the throughput of information is correspondingly degraded.

[94] Generally the use of poly-A means that particular mRNA is destined for use in the cytoplasm. For details, see (e.g.) *Molecular Cell Biology*, 283.

[95] But he that entereth in by the door is the shepherd of the sheep. To him the porter openeth: and the sheep hear his voice. And he calleth his own sheep by name and leadeth them out. And when he hath let out his own sheep, he goeth before them: and *the sheep follow him, because they know his voice.* But a stranger they follow not, but fly from him, because *they know not the voice of strangers.* John 10:2-5, emphasis added.

its sender. This is not a precise statement of a communications method in networking, but it is suggestive. Imagine, if you will, a radio show, a disk-jockey playing music or reciting monologues – the radio engineer may give him the thumbs up that his signal is going out, but how does he know if *anyone* is listening? He cannot – unless someone "calls in" with a request or a complaint. Even in the pre-radio age, the point was known to editors of newspapers:

> The whole modern world is pining for a genuinely sensational journalism. This has been discovered by that very able and honest journalist, Mr. Blatchford, who started his campaign against Christianity, warned on all sides, I believe, that it would ruin his paper, but who continued from an honourable sense of intellectual responsibility. He discovered, however, that while he had undoubtedly shocked his readers, he had also greatly advanced his newspaper. It was bought – first, by all the people who agreed with him and wanted to read it; and secondly, by all the people who disagreed with him, and wanted to write him letters. Those letters were voluminous (I helped, I am glad to say, to swell their volume), and they were generally inserted with a generous fulness. Thus was accidentally discovered (like the steam-engine) the great journalistic maxim – that if an editor can only make people angry enough, they will write half his newspaper for him for nothing.[96]

It is easy enough to see how a communications failure – even a natural one, like someone sneezing during a conversation – can drop a word, even a critical word, and turn a truth into a falsehood. Even one letter can change so much: a major heresy stems from the "iota of difference" between *homoousion* and *homoiousion*. But it occurs in English as well: "It is **now** time to act" versus "It is **not** time to act." In no other passage of scripture do we see our high-technology presaged by Our Lord as when He says, "For amen I say unto you, till heaven and earth pass, one jot, or one tittle shall not pass of the law, till all be fulfilled."[97] The modern form, "the smallest letter, or the smallest part of a letter" is fulfilled in the bits (the smallest part of a byte, the memory unit which can store one letter or digit) by which letters and numbers are represented in ASCII. In such an electronic form, errors of omission are not distinguished from those of commission.

But what about the other kinds of faulty communications, where the messages are more insidious falsehoods, or are generated spuriously? Machines neither lie nor tell the truth – but men can and do lie: they may alter their words from fear or greed or malevolence. How does the purpose (at the individual level) affect communication – especially if that purpose is contrary to the Purpose of the system? Specifically, we might ask how can a superior come to know *the truth* regarding the needs of the inferiors? Likewise, how are the inferiors protected against wrongful action by a

---

[96] GKC, *Heretics* CW1:99-100.
[97] Mt 5:18.

superior? This is a very difficult matter, but it is simplified by our study of a limited mechanical system. Indeed, the simple truth that a machine cannot have a "purpose" of its own helps reveal a number of aspects which are all too easy to overlook when it comes to the human element.

Foremost among these is the idea of "monitoring" – by which I do not mean some intrusive scheme like "Big Brother" in Orwell's *1984*, but rather the natural awareness revealed in countless examples through human history. The famous "Parable of Lazarus and the Rich Man" (Lk 16:19-31) might have been told just to highlight the point I am trying to make. The rich man *knew* about Lazarus: he was aware of him, for he mentions his name specifically to Abraham (Lk 16:23-24). We are not going to pursue the related issues here: my point is that the rich man didn't have to have security cameras or detailed financial records about Lazarus. He didn't need "WATCHER" or such tools; Lazarus "lay at his gate" and so he could see him frequently. This is all the more "monitoring" I mean. We don't need detailed reports about things which are right under our noses – but neither dare we close our eyes to them!

To revert to my example: if the Operator wasn't in the Control Room, the warnings from WATCHER or CUSTOS[98] would have no effect. Yes, the monitoring we require of machinery might be considered intrusive if we were applying it to humans. But there are a variety of techniques for gathering details, and many are not "intrusive" at all. In the end, we must remember, as the rich man didn't: it's not intrusive monitoring to notice something you all but trip over, just outside your front door. And in many cases this natural awareness is all that is required.

Some concluding remarks about Failure

I began this chapter with a little episode of how I was awakened in the middle of the night to solve a problem with our ad insertion system. Such events occur in a multitude of settings, whether the problem be medical or personal or practical, whether the aid requires police or firefighting or plumbers. Somehow, the medical analogy seems to fit best, because of the incredible challenges from the failures possible within the complex system called the human body – but there are well-known steps to be followed: examination of the symptoms, diagnosis, and treatment. In the ad insertion system, our procedure might be called detection, resolution, and prevention – the last being our on-going adjustments of the system to attempt to reduce or prevent the reoccurrence of such failures, or if that is not possible, to augment our system as possible to provide better means of detecting such problems, and better documentation on how to treat them. Such forward-looking studies require another kind of study called *etiology*: this means a

---

[98] CUSTOS was the special monitoring program which watched the machinery of the Home Cluster, in particular making sure that critical programs like PUMP were running. It had a somewhat humorous appearance with "eyes" that shifted back and forth, indicating its own activity; it also could produce audible alerts for critical situations.

study of the *cause* of the problem. As Virgil said, "Happy is he who is able to know the causes of things."[99] As we shall see when we examine the role of virtues in Subsidiarity, knowledge about the Purpose ranks first.

---

[99] "*Felix qui potuit cognoscere causas rerum.*" Virgil, *Georgics*, Book II.

Chapter 5
Extensions of Subsidiarity

As if the topic of Subsidiarity was not complex enough, we must now take up the matter of its extension! There are two meanings to the idea of an "extension" of Subsidiarity. The first is simply an extension of the Purpose of the system, which means some allowance may have to be made in dealing with competing sub-purposes. The second arises from the fact that a human being is a "universal" operator – he can perform a vast range of actions, take on a vast range of roles, and yet be the same person. The man may be a husband and father, be a resident in a city, state and country, attend church, work in business, belong to a club, play sports, and so forth – and each of these "systems" involves him in different circumstances, with different (sometimes conflicting) rules and priorities, and where his needs may vary – sometimes he will require assistance, sometimes he will provide assistance.

Extension of Purpose

I can provide two interesting examples from my experience where we extended our ad insertion system to serve additional purposes. The first was a variation on the idea of a headend, wherein a small television station wanted to have an arrangement by which it could play infomercials (these are 30-minute long advertising shows) during the times when they were not transmitting their usual signals. Our machinery could handle this additional task easily – except for one detail. The infomercials were huge, using over a gigabyte[100] of storage. We could transport them manually over the satellite, but the speed limitations meant that the regular work of ad insertion would be unduly delayed. So we altered PUMP to prevent it from transporting such gigantic files. Subsidiarity worked in exactly the same way – except that now there were files which were "to be sent" which PUMP could not send! Instead, Operations informed Field Services, and one of the Field Techs were dispatched to drive to that site, transporting the infomercials by what is sometimes called "sneaker net." To put it simply, transport of the infomercials were handled as a low-priority task. Such priority schemes are necessary in mechanical systems; the difficulties of managing such things in human societies can be observed in such bottlenecks as the "Express Checkout Lanes" in supermarkets, or in fact in any such queueing scheme.[101] Other complexities occur in cases like dispatch of police or firefighting resources[102], or in the triage (from the French for picking, sorting, selection)

---

[100] A gigabyte is 10^9 or 1,000,000,000 bytes, which sounds huge – but in 2012 one can go into a store and buy a disk drive storing a thousand gigabytes (a terabyte), or even more.

[101] Advanced texts on operating systems design provide details on queues and their behavior.

[102] My brother, a 9-1-1 dispatcher, informed me that in some cases a fire department team will have a pair of firemen specifically allocated to assist the others, which is a perfect miniature of the ancient Roman form of Subsidiarity.

performed in emergency rooms.

The second example occurred when management required us to use our transport system to deliver a variety of files for another form of television presentation. Another computer (which was *not* an inserter) was joined to the subtree, and the transport system was altered to pass these special files to that machine. These files were all handled by our "packaging" technique, and arranged so that this additional duty resulted in no interference with the work of ad insertion. The importance of this example is to demonstrate the idea that the intermediaries must maintain a degree of disinterestedness, displaying a trustworthiness to handle matters on behalf of the lower levels whom they are assisting.

In both cases there is a sense of *priority* assigned to these additional duties. The overall Purpose is enlarged to include several sub-Purposes, and a priority is established in order to resolve any possible conflicts which can arise.

Extension of System

I keep using this word "system" even when I mean a collection of people – as if somehow I am suggesting that a human group is as mechanical as a bunch of computers. No; I know rather more about computing – though we might well ask why is a computer is so human? Not because of its abilities, of course, which are nothing more than a handful of simple mechanical mathematics – but because in a simple sense, the computer has a certain universality to its abilities. It can be given software to have it perform almost any task. In the same way, a human can learn to perform almost any task – though unlike computers, any given human can have a far greater aptitude (or difficulty) with any specific task. Computers are neither lazy nor enthusiastic; they do not get bored or delighted depending on their assignments. But in the ancient Greek sense of *system*, which means *things which are placed together*, humans can cooperate – that is work with others in pursuit of a goal or purpose. A computer can sometimes handle multiple purposes, up to its level of efficiency. But a given person may handle a wide variety of purposes, beyond the ability of any machine, and so may be a part of multiple *systems* of humans, handling a variety of purposes.

Subsidiarity must somehow accommodate this overlapping of systems – one's family, one's religion, one's employment, one's civic, social, recreational groups – and it can. The puzzle we face in such a set of overlapping systems, with their multi-layered scheme of Purpose, is to know how Subsidiarity imposes its order – specifically, *who* is the "superior" one appeals to. In many cases, common sense will suffice: the particular need will indicate the appropriate source of assistance: For example, a priest does not appeal to his bishop when his sink springs a leak, and a police officer does not call a plumber for backup during a bank robbery.

In ambiguous cases, or when common sense is not enough, the strategy is the same as we saw in the previous discussion. There must be a kind of priority which resolves any conflicts among the various purposes, since some things are more important than others. This strategy was given in a classic form in these famous words: "And Jesus said to them: Render therefore to Caesar the things that are Caesar's: and to God the things that are God's."[103] We should note that the determination of this priority is not properly the role of Subsidiarity in itself: common sense and ordinary intelligence ought to suffice in most cases, yet there may be cases requiring careful study, or where guidance must be sought. (Remember, the rules of algebra do not in themselves dictate how they are to apply in any given word-problem!)[104]

---

[103] Lk. 20:25

[104] This is another kind of "incompleteness" of Algebra, recalling the great Incompleteness Theorem of Kurt Gödel and others – but it was already suggested by Cardinal Newman (see the quote on pp. 50-51 above). Indeed, Newman's "Incompleteness Theorem" encompasses every branch of the Circle of Knowledge: we might state it thus: "*Every* branch of knowledge is *incomplete* without *all* others."

Chapter 6
Some Thoughts About Necessary Virtues

Man is a contradiction in terms; he is a beast whose superiority to other beasts consists in having fallen.

GKC, *The Ball and the Cross*, CW7:42

This chapter is quite different from the rest of the book. It is not intended to state or explain something about Subsidiarity, but to give you a little of the thoughts which I have had as I have pondered the topic. As I said in the introduction, Subsidiarity is a paradox: it is almost too simple to describe, and almost too complex to contain within just one book. Its mathematics might be considered as a straightforward arrangement by a "layered" *order* (also called a hierarchy) of *abilities* (or specialized resources) to balance out the *limitations* in pursuit of some *purpose*. ("OPAL" for short.) But as I also indicated, such a view could be nothing more than a blueprint for a machine, or software for a computer (or set of computers), until we remember that there are humans in the system. And thus we face a far greater paradox: for humans are failure-prone in ways which no machine can ever imitate, and humans are superabundant in resourcefulness beyond any natural entity whatsoever. As usual, Chesterton has captured both of these aspects in succinct word-pictures:

[Man] is something else, something strange and solitary; and more like the statue that was once the god of the garden; but the statue has fallen from its pedestal and lies broken among the plants and weeds.[105]

...all that excellent machinery which is the swiftest thing on earth in saving human labour is also the slowest thing on earth in resisting human interference. It may be easier to get chocolate for nothing out of a shopkeeper than out of an automatic machine. But if you did manage to steal the chocolate, the automatic machine would be much less likely to run after you. [106]

But I cannot attempt to summarize all of anthropological morality here. There are textbooks on moral theology,[107] just as there are entire courses in medical school on disease and variety of ways in which the complex system of the human body can fail. It is hard enough, even in a mechanical system, to enumerate the ways by which an inserter might fail – we have presented a handful which are instructive, though obviously there are many others.[108] But after having pondered these, I wish to approach our study from the other side, and point out some of the necessary *virtues*, or human powers, which must be brought to bear upon a system when it is founded upon Subsidiarity.

---

[105] GKC, *The Thing* CW3:311
[106] GKC, *The Ball and the Cross* CW7:211-2
[107] See e.g. the famous *Handbook of Moral Theology* by Dominic M. Prümmer, O.P.
[108] "It is always simple to fall; there are an infinity of angles at which one falls, only one at which one stands." GKC, *Orthodoxy*, CW1:306

We must recall that the fundamental character of our system is the tree, but upside down, suggesting the pyramid founded upon a large number of individuals. So, contrary to the designs of most other historical social systems, Subsidiarity acknowledges, indeed requires that the *individual* is the most important part of the system:

> And the king answering shall say to them: Amen I say to you, as long as you did it to one of these my least brethren, you did it to me. [109]
>
> There is in that [the birth of Christ] alone the touch of a revolution, as of the world turned upside down. It would be vain to attempt to say anything adequate, or anything new, about the change which this conception of a deity born like an outcast or even an outlaw had upon the whole conception of law and its duties to the poor and outcast. It is profoundly true to say that after that moment there could be no slaves. There could be and were people bearing that legal title until the Church was strong enough to weed them out, but there could be no more of the pagan repose in the mere advantage to the state of keeping it a servile state. Individuals became important, in a sense in which no instruments can be important. A man could not be a means to an end, at any rate to any other man's end. [110]
>
> For religion all men are equal, as all pennies are equal, because the only value in any of them is that they bear the image of the King. [111]

For Subsidiarity, the importance to the system always increases as one descends through the levels of the organization, and it decreases as one ascends. The powers of the individual, then, are to be preserved, safeguarded, and extended whenever possible, for Subsidiarity is about assistance where it does the most good. More than any other single virtue, then, the individual must have *knowledge*: knowledge of the structure of the system, of its purpose, the limitations and resources. [112]

Yes, there is a risk involved: individuals may fail. This happens, and it must be allowed for in the planning of the order of the system. [113] But in real

---

[109] Mt 25:40

[110] GKC *The Everlasting Man* CW2:305.

[111] GKC *Charles Dickens* CW15:44.

[112] Here we see the formal inversion of Tennyson's epigram: "Theirs not to reason why, Theirs but to do and die," a heinous anti-Christian, because anti-human viewpoint.

[113] It is interesting to note, from our example that the lowest orders are in some sense "fungible" – that is, a leaf or portal might be replaced by another of the same type and handle the work as well – at the same time, the higher in the order, the less "replaceable" is that component. It would be much harder to replace HOME than a

human societies, there are also those individuals, to be found at every level, who will "go the extra mile"[114] or (in the ludicrous sports phrase) "give 110%" – such supernatural qualities can be expected to arise in a human society as long as they have not been excluded by ignorance, neglect, or malevolence. This is mirrored precisely in the mechanical analogies we have described, for computers must be programmed, and machines must be built to spec, if these tools are to play their roles. (That is, full knowledge of their roles must exist in a programmer, designer, or mechanic, in order that the device may function properly.) Thus *knowledge* must rank first in our list of virtues:

1. **Knowledge**: The individual must *know* the purpose of the system, and his own role in achieving it.[115] Natural limitations or unexpected events will require an associated virtue, in order that this work not cease:

2. **Courage**:[116] The individual must steadfastly perform his role in working toward the purpose, despite whatever obstacles may arise, whether they are external, relating to the work at hand, or internal to the worker (like boredom). Yet such obstacles may indicate a task beyond his power, so in order to correctly judge in such cases, he will require:

3. **Prudence**: He must be aware of limitations (either inherent in him, or in the role he plays, or in the resources available) and recognize when a situation demands courage, and when it demands appeal to higher authority. This virtue, in turn, necessitates another virtue:

4. **Humility**: I have stressed the importance of knowledge to Subsidiarity, and in this unexpected place it is essential. Here, humility means knowing one's place.[117] It means (on one hand) knowing when the task exceeds one's ability, and (on the other hand) knowing when one has the special skills or abilities or knowledge of the situation to be able to handle something, even despite counsel (sometimes inappropriate) from superiors. Nor is this virtue limited to those at the lowest level: it may be the case that the request is beyond the abilities of the superior, and he can do nothing more than pass on the appeal to his own superior. Hence we require two

---

leaf or portal, and all but impossible to replace the big dish, which was a "single point of failure" in our case. But then we also see such complexities in the account of the authority of Moses passing on to Joshua. (See the conclusion of Deuteronomy and the beginning of the book of Joshua.)

[114] Cf. Mt 5:41.

[115] Thus Tennyson is inverted: if I must do and I must die, then I *must* know the reason why. Little wonder *Knowledge* is a gift of the Holy Spirit. Also recall the second question in the Catechism: "Why did God make me? God made me to *know* Him, love Him, and serve Him in this world, and be happy with him in the next."

[116] Clearly *Fortitude* plays a role here, just as *Wisdom* in the previous item and *Counsel* in the next.

[117] GKC: Pride consists in a man making his personality the only test, instead of making the truth the test. It is not pride to wish to do well, or even to look well, according to a real test. It is pride to think that a thing looks ill, because it does not look like something characteristic of oneself. GKC, "If I Only Had One Sermon to Preach" in *The Common Man* 254.

converging virtues:

5. **Trust** and

6. **Honesty**: Subsidiarity is impossible without communication, and the communication of non-truths is only noise. Assistance can be predicated only upon an accurate expression of the need in the situation at hand – and assistance must be reliably provided when appeal is made.

Finally, related to these attributes of communication is:

7. **Obedience**: Often the appeal to a superior for the satisfaction of a need will induce new tasks, usually for the one seeking assistance, sometimes for others as well. These new tasks must be performed as ordered, for they are part of the Purpose; perhaps even more richly so, as such tasks involve a larger operation within the system.

We might summarize all these virtues into the single term *co-operation*, not in the merely literal sense of *working together*, but with the deeper quality of friendly harmony, of teamwork, of the thrill that runs through an orchestra in the final chord of a symphony. Yet this quality is within the individual. As I noted above, these qualities are not restricted to those on the lowest level. They apply, sometimes with greater force and with more poignant subtlety, to those on the higher levels: "And unto whomsoever much is given, of him much shall be required."[118] In this fashion, the system is no longer a collection of separate entities, but *one* – and thus is more perfectly brought to bear upon its purpose. Subsidiarity is the best way, the way most fitting to the human condition, by which this unity can be brought about. For, as philosophy teaches, "a thing is more perfect as it is more perfectly one." [119]

---

[118] Lk 12:48
[119] Kreyche, *First Philosophy*, 175.

Chapter 7
Some Additional Points About Designing a System

Since Subsidiarity is a most general approach to organization, it can be applied to comparatively small arrangements as well as large ones. We might call it a "three-body problem" for all of the issues we have discussed come into play only when there are at least three components to the system, and not just two. But Subsidiarity is completely scaleable, and extends to systems of any size or complexity, limited only by the ingenuity of the system-designer and the resources at hand.

In fact, since a smaller system will generally be simpler, it is easier to consider more of the issues involved. (That is why I have spent so many pages explaining ad insertion.) Hence, I will point out some additional "systems design" issues which may help in applying Subsidiarity to situations where the system is not yet constructed.

First, one ought to apply the OPAL scheme: Order, Purpose, Ability, and Limitation. Sure, there are various techniques for laying out such designs; each branch of engineering has methods for stating such designs. But you should also take advantage of the work of others when you can – you are striving to achieve a purpose in the real world, not do a school project, so it will be beneficial to see what the other disciplines have to offer.

Then one should consider the kinds of failure which can occur, whether these failures are "correctable" in a simple sense by a straightforward appeal for assistance, or whether there is something "fatal" in which components need to be replaced. Closely related to this task is the need to provide communication pathways which permit appeals for help as well as detection of failures, bearing in mind that those pathways can also fail. Here, there are two axioms which can assist you:

1) Juvenal: "Who will watch the watchers themselves?"[120] Remember the importance of communication, demanding both honesty and trust.

2) Anastomosis: provide for alternate pathways, especially at critical junctions. There are remarkably few paths in the circulatory system which are absolutely singular and essential. If your system demands such 24/7 stability, you will need to design comparable redundancies into it.

When one wants to apply Subsidiarity to an existing system, that system must be studied carefully so as not to be trapped by the "illusion of hierarchy" in the system. The correct hierarchy must be sought according to the Purpose, and is not necessarily the obvious one: for example, it is probably not visible in the company "org chart." One needs to have the true scientific spirit, which is humility before the Real World, to discover the truth about it. Always build your pyramid starting from the bottom.

Moreover, it should be noted that even in comparatively small systems, there can be more than one purpose, and so there has to be multiple and even

---

[120] Satire VI. These words in the original Latin, actually appeared on the WATCHER screens in the Control Room.

overlapping applications of the scheme. Such complexity requires great precision in stating the Purpose at hand, and the management of competing needs for scarce resources will follow according to that Purpose.

Finally, if there is one virtue which strongly stands out as essential for a system designer, it is humility, which we see in God Himself, Who "emptied Himself, taking the form of a servant."[121] The "niche" for each component must be considered: its place in the system, its abilities and its limitations, its communication paths. As we have seen, the lowest members are the most important, and the designer must "know" them in their places, even if he does not actually perform those tasks himself.

The Mystery of Subsidiarity

In the introduction I mentioned the famous story of the Wedding Feast at Cana where the wine ran out: the three levels, an appeal from the lowest level for assistance, an appeal at a higher level; directives issued and the need fulfilled. Now, perhaps, if you have struggled to understand a little of what I have struggled to present to you, this mystery may be illuminated somewhat. But it is still a true *mystery*, not a puzzle for detectives to solve, but a light for us to walk by:

> The mystic allows one thing to be mysterious, and everything else becomes lucid. ... The one created thing which we cannot look at is the one thing in the light of which we look at everything. Like the sun at noonday, mysticism explains everything else by the blaze of its own victorious invisibility. [122]

Or perhaps you might prefer a more ancient source:

> Truly, I see it not [this light of God], because it is too bright for me. And yet, whatsoever I see, I see through it, as the weak eye sees what it sees through the light of the sun, which in the sun itself it cannot look upon.[123]

Perhaps this mystical hint will only be confusing to those who expect a more technical discussion. But perhaps, after some meditation, it will be the answer to any number of difficulties:

"Do whatever He tells you." [124]

---

[121] Ph 2:7
[122] GKC, *Orthodoxy*, CW1:231
[123] *The Proslogion* of St. Anselm, chapter 16.
[124] See Jn 2:5

Chapter 8
Conclusion: Technical Love

It is a "principle of overwhelming *practical* application" that "a thing is more perfect as it is more perfectly one."[125] In fact, Subsidiarity is really just a corollary of this idea. For Subsidiarity is about the *order* in a system working towards a *purpose* – an order which strives to make possible the achievement of that purpose in the most common-sense way – to set the various parts working, each according to its speciality as well as its limitations, with the idea that the need of one can be satisfied by another, providing that need is communicated along an orderly path.

It is not simply a matter of being helpful. It is an *orderly helpfulness.* Remember that the ancient Roman army didn't merely have back-up soldiers – that would have merely been a second layer. They had a *third layer* of assistants, and they had *order* which meant that the assistance would be effective. (See Lk 7:8) Sure, it gets technical. But it works!

That is why I call this conclusion "Technical Love." It is a challenge to our fallen human nature to "love your neighbor as yourself,"[126] though the "Golden Rule" points out that we must treat others as we would wish to be treated.[127] This is fundamental, but even in the simplest of societies, or in facing the most bland of practical problems, something more detailed is required. The shortest way of stating this essential is *wisdom*: there must be something which organizes: "It belongs to wisdom to set things in order."[128] This is what Subsidiarity is: it is *technical love* – a matter of practice, of implementation, according to justice as well as according to charity. Indeed, it is *overwhelmingly practical.*

By this means, the system is *united* in the accomplishment of the purpose: it is *made one.* The athlete calls it teamwork. A Frenchman calls it *esprit de corps.* A businessman relies on the same Latin root and calls it a *corporation*, though as yet few have committed themselves to Subsidiarity, at least on a large scale. The anatomist calls it the human body. The Church (keeping St. Paul's analogy in mind) calls it the Mystical Body. It can apply to any body...

And Subsidiarity is the way in which its perfection is to be pursued.

---

[125] Kreyche, *First Philosophy*, 175, emphasis added.
[126] Lev. 19:18; Mt 22:39.
[127] Lk 6:31
[128] St. Thomas Aquinas, *Summa Theologica* II-II Q45 A6 quoting Aristotle, *Metaphysics* I:2

Appendix 1

Spot Transport for Ad Insertion
A Technical Statement

Note: I have inserted this appendix for the sake of completeness. If you do not know set theory you can skip this portion without losing anything. Everything here is just a formal mathematical way of saying what I said in Part II of this book.

The following is a brief formal statement of the solution of the spot transport problem. Note that a large number of practical matters (which are required in a real implementation) have been omitted.

A. Definitions

1. $\mathbf{N}$ is the set of networks on which ad insertion is to be performed.

2. $\mathbf{H}$ is the set of headends where insertion occurs.

3. For each headend h in $\mathbf{H}$, the set $\mathbf{N}(h)$ is a subset of $\mathbf{N}$, specifying the networks h inserts on.

4. $\mathbf{I}$ is the set of inserters, devices performing insertion for headends.

5. Every inserter i in $\mathbf{I}$ belongs to a certain headend h specified by $\mathrm{H}(i)$.

6. The inserters for a given headend h are the set $\mathbf{I}(h)$ where
   $\mathbf{I}(h) = \{i \mid i \in \mathbf{I} \text{ and } \mathrm{H}(i)=h\}$

Note that $\mathbf{I}$ is *partitioned* among the headends: that is,
   $(1) \quad \bigcup_{h \in \mathbf{H}} \mathbf{I}(h) = \mathbf{I}$
and
   (2) for any $x, y \in \mathbf{H}$ with $x \neq y$, we have $\mathbf{I}(x) \cap \mathbf{I}(y) = \varnothing$

7. An inserter i performs insertion on a set $\mathbf{N}(i)$ of networks. Note that the networks of h are *partitioned* among the inserters: that is,
   $(1) \quad \bigcup_{i \in \mathbf{I}(h)} \mathbf{N}(i) = \mathbf{N}(h)$
and
   (2) for any $x, y \in \mathbf{I}(h)$ with $x \neq y$, we have $\mathbf{N}(x) \cap \mathbf{N}(y) = \varnothing$

8. For each headend h, there is one and only one distinguished inserter P(h) in **I**(h), called the *portal* for that headend.

9. We define *isportal*(i) to be **true** if i is a portal, **false** otherwise.

10. **M** is the set of names of presently known spots (M for MPEG).

11. Headquarters keeps the MASTER LIBRARY of all spots presently encoded and available for play, noted as the state variable **MasterLib**, a subset of **M**.

12. Each inserter i has a library of spots, noted as the state variable **Lib**(i) which is a subset of **M**, indicating which spots are present and therefore playable at that inserter.

13. A schedule entry is a pair $<m,t>$ where the spot m is a member of **M** and t is a time; this means that at time t the spot m is to be inserted. (Note m may not presently be encoded, or even exist, except as a name.)

14. A schedule **s** for a given headend, network, and date, written as **s**(h,n,d), is defined to be a set of schedule entries $\{<m,t>\}$. This indicates that spot m is to be inserted on headend h, network n at time t on date d. (Note that a large number of technical details and restrictions relating to spot use, times, windows, and cues are omitted here.)

15. A given inserter i has a state variable **S**(i) which is the set of all schedules it has at present:
$$\mathbf{S}(i) = \{\mathbf{s}(\mathbf{H}(i),n,d) \mid n \in \mathbf{N}(i) \text{ and } d \text{ is not past}\}$$
Note, for our purposes, only schedules for the present and future are in **S**.

16. Spot use: for a given inserter i, **Use**(i) is a state variable defined to be the set of spots in use by any present and future schedule for that inserter.
$$\mathbf{Use}(i) = \{ m \mid <m,t> \in \mathbf{s} \text{ and } \mathbf{s} \in \mathbf{S}(i) \}$$

17. The have-spots list: for a given inserter i, **Have**(i) is a state variable defined to be the spots actually present on that inserter, regardless of whether they are actually being used by a schedule.
$$\mathbf{Have}(i) = \mathbf{Lib}(i)$$

18. The needed-spots list: for a given inserter i, **Need**(i) is a state variable defined to be the spots in use, but not present on that inserter.
$$\mathbf{Need}(i) = \mathbf{Use}(i) - \mathbf{Have}(i).$$
Note this is a *set difference*, which can also be represented as:
$$\mathbf{Need}(i) = \{ m \mid m \in \mathbf{Use}(i) \text{ and } m \notin \mathbf{Have}(i)\}$$

19. The portal spot request: for a given headend h, $\mathbf{PSR}(h)$ is a state variable defined to be the set of spots needed by at least one inserter in h but present on no inserter of h:

$\mathbf{PSR}(h) = \mathbf{Need}(h) - \mathbf{Have}(h)$

where

$\mathbf{Need}(h) = \cup \ \mathbf{Need}(i)$
$\qquad\quad i \in \mathbf{I}(h)$

and

$\mathbf{Have}(h) = \cup \ \mathbf{Have}(i)$
$\qquad\quad i \in \mathbf{I}(h)$

Again this set difference can also be represented as:

$\mathbf{PSR}(h) = \{ \ m \mid m \in \mathbf{Need}(h) \text{ and } m \notin \mathbf{Have}(h)\}$

Now we have all the necessary items to specify the processes.

B. The Subsidiarity Process for a Portal

For a given inserter i, if *isportal*(i), perform tasks 1 and 2 independently:

Task 1. Whenever either state variable $\mathbf{S}(i)$ or $\mathbf{Lib}(i)$ changes, recompute $\mathbf{Need}(i)$ and $\mathbf{Have}(i)$ and send them to P(H(i)).

Task 2. Whenever a new $\mathbf{Need}(z)$ or $\mathbf{Have}(z)$ is received by i:

a. Perform Subsidiarity at the portal level.
   For each spot m which is **both** in $\mathbf{Need}(j)$ for some j in $\mathbf{I}(H(i))$
   and in $\mathbf{Have}(k)$ for some k in $\mathbf{I}(H(i))$:
   Perform the transport of m from k to j.

The meaning is that spot m exists on k and is needed by j which does not have it: the portal "satisfies the need" by performing the transport. Note that upon completion of the transport, $\mathbf{Lib}(j)$ will change, which will cause the generation of a new $\mathbf{Need}(j)$ and $\mathbf{Have}(j)$, but now m will be in $\mathbf{Have}$, and *not* in $\mathbf{Need}$.

b. Recompute $\mathbf{PSR}(H(i))$ and send it to HOME, which will invoke Subsidiarity there.

C. The Subsidiarity Process for a non-Portal

For a given inserter i, if NOT *isportal*(i):

Whenever either state variable $S(i)$ or $Lib(i)$ changes, recompute **Need**(i) and **Have**(i) and send them to P(H(i)). Note that if **Need**(i) is not empty, Subsidiarity will be invoked at the portal.

D. The Subsidiarity Process at HOME

The process at HOME is similar to that for a portal, and works like this:

Whenever a new **PSR** is received, or when the MASTER LIBRARY changes:

1. Compute the "**FieldNeed**" List – this is the set of spots needed by all headends in the Field:

FieldNeed $= \cup$ **PSR**(h)
$ h \in$ **H**

2. Compute the "To Be Sent" List – this is the set of spots existing in the MASTER LIBRARY and are to be sent to the headends needing them:

$\qquad$ **ToBeSent** = FieldNeed $\cap$ **MasterLib**

3. Compute the "To Be Encoded" List – this is the set of spots needed by some headends but not in the MASTER LIBRARY, so they must be encoded:
$\qquad$ **ToBeEncoded** = FieldNeed – MasterLib

Note this is a *set difference*, which can also be represented as:
$\qquad$ **ToBeEncoded** = { $m \mid m \in$ **FieldNeed** and $m \notin$ **MasterLib**}

4. Perform Subsidiarity at HOME:

$\qquad$ For each spot m in **ToBeSent**,
$\qquad\qquad$ Perform transport of m to every portal p where $m \in$ **PSR**(H(p)).

Note that this will change **Lib**(p), which will invoke Subsidiarity on that portal, causing generation of a new **PSR**, and so forth.

E. The Subsidiarity Process at Operations

The operator in the Control Room uses the **ToBeEncoded** list to organize the priorities of encoding. When a new spot is encoded, it is placed into the MASTER LIBRARY, which invokes Subsidiarity on HOME.

Note: In practice, the Operations department had various policies which specified what was to be done when discrepancies or difficulties arose with encoding, when a spot was missing, machine failure, and so forth.

Appendix 2

An Abstraction of Subsidiarity

Now that you have been on a little tour of our (alas!) vanished technique for spot transport for local ad insertion of cable TV, it is time for me to attempt an *abstract* description of Subsidiarity. That is, one that doesn't have spots or headends in it.

Note: I will use certain ideas or symbolisms from set theory, but I will not proceed into the mathematical rigor as I did in Appendix 1, since this abstraction can only be specified in very general terms. Anyway, it is a starting point, and if it is ever dealt with by experts, perhaps they will get further into the necessary formalisms.

1. Starting Axioms
In order to make this abstraction, we start with a series of axioms about the realm in which we are going to act.

Axiom 1. There is *something which needs to be done.* This is the *purpose* we call **P**. This purpose might be singular, that is once-and-done, as in the winning of a sporting event, or it may be continuous, that is on-going, as in ad insertion.

Axiom 2. There are *a collection of individuals* which we call **I**. Typically these are human beings, but there is no inherent reason *not* to consider other kinds of individuals such as machines. (According to the "Jaki Restriction," Subsidiarity is strictly limited to human beings; see my earlier discussion on this.) By the specification of ancient Rome, it is understood that there are at least three individuals.

Axiom 3. These individuals form, or at least can be considered as, a *system* **S**. (We'll see some details about that system shortly.)

Axiom 4. In order to accomplish the purpose **P**, a variety of *tasks* **T** must be performed. For the sake of this abstraction, we'll assume that each individual i in **I** must perform a certain task t in order for the Purpose to be accomplished. This task is performed by the individual: maybe only once at the right time, or repeatedly, according to whatever may be necessary to the attaining of the Purpose. For example, two different individuals, say you and I, both work at accomplishing our purpose **P**, but our tasks may not be at all similar. We could both do the same task (perhaps at different locations), or we might both do different tasks, but both tasks are somehow necessary to the accomplishment of **P**.

2. The Hierarchy for Subsidiarity

Considering the general arrangement of things, unless the Purpose is comparatively simple (or complex), only *some* of the tasks will actually accomplish the Purpose. Let us say that the (set of) individuals who perform those tasks are called I_0. We can presume that the natural arrangement of our system S is to have this set maximized.

Obviously the details of the arrangement depend on the purpose, but there is one common element which I will address next. Also, I must point out that "as many" does not mean the strict mathematical "maximization" of I_0 – for example, only one person on a football team can have the football at once! It should be understood in a simpler sense: as many I_0 are "involved" in the accomplishment of P as the nature of the situation may permit (that is, no one is idling unnecessarily).

Under some conditions, we shall presume that someone in I_0 needs assistance; he turns to another individual, who (for that very reason) is considered to be in a collection I_1 of "first-level assistants."

Then under some conditions, let us say that someone in I_1 needs assistance; he turns to another individual – as above, that one is considered to be in a collection I_2 of "second-level assistants."

And so forth, as high as may be necessary, or permitted, by the nature of the system and individuals and problem being considered. Remember that any given individual might serve on more than one level, depending on the nature of the things involved.

This is a very rough sketch, barely enough to suggest the tree-nature of the structure, but the shape ought to be clear from our example.

3. Some Observations

Now, this is hardly a complete description of Subsidiarity even compared to the rather technical discussion I presented in the first Appendix. But except for adding another bunch of symbols to indicate the various forms of "appeals" between the levels, there really is not very much more to define.

But I have tried to indicate that Subsidiarity is actually a very simple, and very commonsense idea, except for one very strange thing: unlike normal hierarchies, we see that the "higher" I_k exist to *serve* the lower orders, not the other way around! Even as we ascend the tree towards greater authorities, to those who resolve larger and more difficult needs, these are compelled to serve the lower orders, in order to achieve the Purpose.

This is a great paradox, and touches on biblical matters. At the Last Supper, Jesus told the Apostles: "Even as the Son of man is not come to be ministered unto, but to minister and to give his life a redemption for many. ... He that is the greatest among you shall be your servant."[129] It also is consistent with the nature of the Papacy, one of the titles of which is "Servant of the servants of God."

---

[129] Mt 20:28, 23:11. Recall "to minister" means "to serve."

Another paradox is that the higher I_k are *comparatively distant* from the tasks which achieve the purpose **P**, even while their roles may be critical to the performance of **P**! In fact, the higher the level, the more remote they are.

However, it means that, in at least a certain sense, the lowest members need to have the greatest awareness of the purpose of the system. This is in direct opposition to Tennyson's epigram about "Theirs not to reason why, Theirs but to do and die." – which might be the motto of anti-Subsidiarity.

Glossary

24/7 (read as "twenty-four, seven") Jargon for something which is active twenty-four hours a day, seven days a week. At our company, Operations was staffed 24/7; the machines of the Home Cluster and the Field were running 24/7. Note: It should come as no surprise that this is biblical in origin: "And you shall not go out of the door of the tabernacle *for seven days*, until the day wherein the time of your consecration shall be expired. For in seven days the consecration is finished ... *Day and night shall you remain in the tabernacle observing the watches of the Lord...*" [Lev. 8:33,35 emphasis added.]

Abusus non tollit usum (Latin; a WATCHER slogan) "Abuse does not take away use."

Ad Insertion the playing of commercials for regional or local clients: this playing overrides the "national" spot which is then being played by the network, so the viewers see the local spot, not the national one.

Ad Sales the department which handles customer requests to have a spot played, or changed, or cancelled. The only department to deal with customers seeking advertising on cable TV. Once a specific request has been made, Ad Sales passes the details on to the Traffic Department.

Afferent nerves which transmits sensory signals; their messages travel *from* a sense organ *towards* the brain or spinal cord.

Anastomosis the union or intercommunication of any system or network; in biology, such a union between hollow vessels such as blood vessels; also called inosculation. "...this communication is very free between the large as well as the smaller branches. The anastomosis between trunks of equal size is found where great activity of the circulation is requisite, as in the brain ... also found in the abdomen. In the limbs the anastomoses are most numerous and of largest size around the joints, the branches of an artery above inosculating with branches from the vessels below; these anastomoses are of considerable interest to the surgeon, as it is by their enlargement that a *collateral circulation* [italics in original] is established after the application of a ligature for the cure of aneurism. The smaller branches of arteries anastomose more frequently than the larger, and between the smallest twigs these inosculations become so numerous as to constitute a *close network* [my italics] that pervades nearly every tissue of the body. [*Gray's Anatomy*, 474]

Aorta the great trunk artery which leaves the heart, the root of all other arteries.

ASCII the acronym for "American Standard Code for Information Interchange" – the very common representation of letters, digits, and punctuation as one of the 256 possible patterns of zero and one in an 8-bit byte.

Artery   a blood vessel within which blood flows *away from* the heart.

Break Short for "commercial break" – that is, a pause or interruption in a television program for the purpose of showing advertising. The breaks are typically one minute in duration, and occur around 28 minutes after the hour and two minutes before the hour. At these times, networks usually permit the insertion of a local or regional advertising spot.

Bit (from *Binary digIT*) the smallest unit of information storage (memory) in a computer, representing either the value "zero" or the value "one" by two distinct voltage levels. (Strikingly referred to by Christ in Mt 5:37.)

Byte an elementary unit of information storage (memory) in a computer, consisting of 8 bits, hence capable of storing any of 256 possible values. As this suffices for a single ASCII character (letter, digit, or punctuation), the term is usually interchangeable with *character*.

Cable Television In our example, a company which supplies various nationally available (and other) television networks to home viewers by means of wires actually strung to individual houses in a given geographical area.

Capillary the tiniest blood vessels where blood supplies oxygen and nutrients to the adjacent tissues, and takes away waste.

Centesimus Annus an encyclical (1991) by John Paul II commemorating the hundredth anniversary of *Rerum Novarum*.

Control Room the room, staffed 24/7, where the Operations department does the monitoring and control of the machinery of both the Field and the Home Cluster, as well as encoding.

Cue-tone [from *cue*, a variant spelling of *Q*, from the Latin *quando* meaning "when"] A signal transmitted by a cable TV network, indicating that a local spot is now permitted to be played. (This signal is not normally available to a home viewer. It sounds like four touch-tone beeps, and occurs a fixed interval of time before the spots may play, usually about five seconds – this interval is called the "preroll" for that network.)

CUSTOS [Latin: the watcher, or guardian] the special monitoring program which watched the machinery of the Home Cluster, in particular making sure that critical programs like PUMP were running. It had a somewhat humorous appearance with "eyes" that shifted back and forth indicating its own activity; it also could produce audible alerts for critical situations.

Custos Packet data generated by the ENGINE running on an inserter in the Field, by which it communicated its status back to Headquarters.

Development the department (together with the Tech Shop) which arranges, tests, and sets up the production machinery for the other departments.

Directory the information on a computer disk which acts as a card catalog indicating the location of the other information on that disk, such as files. If it is a hierarchial directory, the information may also be additional directories (called "subdirectories") or files of various kinds.

Disk drive the "permanent memory" of a computer, where information is stored under control of a program. Generally a disk can be considered to contain three things: (1) a number of files containing information of one kind or another; (2) a directory (often a hierarchical file system) which has information about the files such as their name, location, size, and so forth; (3) free space not in use by a file or directory. Unlike the "working memory," the disk memory is preserved while the computer is off, but it is much slower to use.

Efferent nerves which transmit control signals; their messages travel *from* the brain or spinal cord *towards* a muscle, gland or other body part.

Encoding the conversion of a TV commercial from its analog form on a magnetic tape into a digitized form (typically MPEG).

Encyclical a document written by a pope intended for world-wide distribution.

ENGINE the computer program running on an inserter which actually accomplishes ad insertion: it controls the playback devices which play the spots out on the proper cable networks at times dictated according to the schedule, and records its work in a log.

Family [from a Latin root meaning servant] the body of persons living in one house, under one head, a household; those descending from a common ancestor; a group of closely related individuals.

FERRY the computer program running on an inserter which handles transport of information: if the inserter is a leaf, between that inserter and the portal of the subtree; if the inserter is a portal, between that inserter and HOME, or between that inserter and any other in the subtree.

Field the collection of all machinery located distant from our Headquarters. The Field is divided into "headends" – the particular installations serving a given region of cable TV viewers, and "inserters" – the machinery at a given headend which do the work of ad insertion.

Field Services the department which handles installation or repair of our machinery in the Field.

File on a computer disk, the fundamental unit of useful information storage.

Geosynchronous orbit a satellite in geosynchronous orbit is revolving around the earth, completing its orbit in exactly one day. Hence, it does not move when viewed from the earth's surface, and so we are able to aim a satellite dish at it for use in communicating with another dish.

Headend a collection of equipment at a particular location in the Field which serves a geographical region of cable TV viewers by providing them with various cable TV networks. One or more inserters may be assigned to a given headend in order to perform ad insertion for those networks.

Headquarters the central location of the company which accomplishes ad insertion for a cable TV provider. Besides the usual corporate offices, it consists of the Ad Sales department which handles customers, and a variety of internal departments such as Traffic, Field Services, and Operations. It also includes various electronic components which do the mechanical work, such as the computers handling the traffic and billing processes and the production machines of the Home Cluster (HOME, the MASTER LIBRARY, the monitors for Operations, encoders and other equipment).

Hierarchy [Greek: sacred leadership] a scheme of ordering or arranging a collection of items by classes, each of which has a level or rank. As a general rule, a hierarchy can be represented as a diagram which looks like a tree with its root at the top, the branches extending downwards until they end in leaves.

Hierarchical File System a scheme of organizing files of information on the disks of a computer. It uses the idea of a *directory* which may contain any number of files, but may also contain *other* directories (usually referred to as "subdirectories"). The outermost directory is called the *root* directory, because the whole collection can be drawn as a tree with the files as leaves, the subdirectories as branches, and the root directory as its "root"(though it is always drawn at the top, not at the bottom).

Histology the branch of biology which studies the kinds of cells and tissues (groups of cells) in an organism, including its physical features and properties, and its relation to other such entities, as well as its origin, functions, and purpose in its anatomical site within the system of the living being.

HOME the main computer of the Home Cluster, which manages all transport of information to or from the Field. The primary program running on HOME is called PUMP.

Home Cluster all the machinery located at Headquarters involved in accomplishing the work of our example.

Inserter a piece of electronic equipment built from a computer, large disk drive, from one to eight "playback" devices, and other components, all treated as a singular entity. It has a "name" which identifies the computer within the networks on which it communicates. The two programs which run on an inserter are FERRY (which does transport) and ENGINE (which does the actual insertion). An inserter is located at a specific headend in the Field.

Juvenal Delinquent one who (like your author) has neglected the reading of the classical writers, and is struggling to catch up.

Leaf in our example, an inserter which is not a portal; it can communicate only with the portal, which handles all communications with the Home Cluster for the machines of that headend.

Local Spot a commercial which is intended to be played only within a certain geographical area. It is *inserted* into the *national feed*, thereby suppressing the *national spot* which would otherwise be visible at that time. A typical network might permit one minute of such spots twice in each hour of the day, thus each day there are usually 96 opportunities to play a 30 second spot for local or regional businesses.

MASTER LIBRARY At Headquarters, a computer with very large-capacity disk drives which stores the encoded spots until they are needed to be transported. It is just a large storage device for spots in their electronic form.

Mater et Magistra encyclical (1961) by Pope John XXIII; it uses the term "principle of subsidiary function" in referring to Pius XI's *Quadragesimo Anno*.

Monitoring someone from the Operations Department periodically checks the state of the various machines, both those at Headquarters and those in the Field.

MPEG [acronym for Motion Picture Engineering Group] In our example, a synonym for a TV commercial, but one which is now *encoded* into a computerized form (called "MPEG-2"), and identified with a *spot ID* (its "file name") for use throughout our equipment. A typical 30-second spot takes up about 20 megabytes when encoded in MPEG-2.

National Feed the actual programming – both shows and commercials – which come directly from a national cable TV network. No local or regional spots will ever be seen on such a feed, as these must be inserted locally, and the national feed is the same across the nation.

National Spot the commercials which play *nationally* on the various cable TV networks. These are usually for large businesses or organizations which are nationwide in their availability or coverage. Generally, a cable TV network permits local cable companies to override some national spots with *local spots*: thus local or regional businesses can buy advertising on such channels.

Nemo dat qui non habet (Latin; a WATCHER slogan) "Nobody gives what he does not have." This epigram of scholastic philosophy is the motto of the transport machinery: for example, PUMP can only transport spots which are already in the MASTER LIBRARY.

Nerve a pathway within a living body through which sensory information or muscular control is transported.

Network There are two uses of this term. When referring to television, a network means a "channel" or "station" which governs its own shows. When referring to computers, a network means a means by which two or more computers may communicate with each other. Loosely speaking, the INTERNET is a public form of a network, but computers can be linked by a network without having any association with the INTERNET.

Operating System a special kind of computer program which runs continuously; its purpose is to permit the computer to be useful by a user or by other programs; it simplifies complex duties such as control of memory, disks and other devices, and including the use of the computer itself.

Operations the department which performs encoding (conversion of tapes to MPEG) and monitoring of the machinery of both the Home Cluster and the Field. This department is a 24/7 operation, that is, someone is always on duty in the Control Room.

Pacem in Terris an encyclical (1963) by Pope John XXIII; it was the first to use the term "subsidiarity" (in paragraph 140).

Playback device in older inserters, the spots were played back by VTRs or VCRs under computer control, so the spots had to be stored on magnetic media, and transport was by hand. In more recent inserters, the playback device is a special component within a computer which has inputs and outputs for both audio and video; the spots are delivered and played in a digital form such as MPEG.

Portal [Latin *porta* = door or gate] the single inserter in a headend which is able to communicate with the Home Cluster; it handles the communications for all the other inserters (leaves) in that headend.

Production Machinery this term distinguishes the machinery being actively used in the direct accomplishment of the company goals, rather than equipment which is being developed or tested, or other company machinery common to any business which is used in the normal activities of running business (calculators, computers used by accounting or finance, for secretarial or management tasks, and so forth).

Program A computer program is a series of special instructions which makes the computer work in a particular way, just as a music roll causes a player piano to perform a particular piece of music. Some of the instructions are "conditional": they are to be performed only in certain circumstances or at certain times.

PUMP A computer program running on the main transport computer (called HOME) at Headquarters. It manages the transport of files going out to the Field, including schedules and MPEGs, and receives files coming from the Field, including logs and requests for needed spots.

Quadragesimo Anno The encyclical (1931) by Pope Pius XI commemorating the fortieth anniversary of *Rerum Novarum*; it contains the first (negative) formulation of the principle of subsidiarity.

Quidquid recipitur in modum recipientis recipitur (Latin; a WATCHER slogan) "Whatever is received is received according to the mode of the receiver " This is an aphorism from scholastic philosophy.

Quis Custodiet Ipsos Custodes? (Latin; a WATCHER slogan) "Who Will Watch the Watchers Themselves?" This famous epigram from Juvenal's Satire VI, written in the first century A.D., points out the dilemma of the monitoring function.

Rerum Novarum The encyclical (1891) by Pope Leo XIII, the first of the so-called modern social teaching documents of the Roman Catholic Church.

Sales Rep (for Sales Representative) a member of the Ad Sales department, who deals with customers wishing to have their TV commercials played.

Satellite a "man-made moon" which is a piece of electronic equipment placed into geosynchronous orbit to serve as a kind of high-tech mirror: it permits certain kinds of radio signals to reach a wider area than would otherwise be possible.

Schedule a list of instructions given to the ENGINE running on an inserter. It specifies the following items: (a) what headend and date it is for; (b) what network it is for; (c) details which specify a time interval and the spots to be played when a cuetone is received during that interval.

Scholastic Philosophy The philosophy brought to a high level of development in Europe during the 12th-13th centuries, exemplified by the work of St. Thomas Aquinas. As Chesterton said, "I revert to the doctrinal methods of the thirteenth century, inspired by the general hope of getting something done." [*Heretics* CW1:46] People were surprised to learn that this is how we got things done at work, and the results were quite satisfactory.

Society [from a Latin root meaning to follow] Loosely, any collection of human beings.

Spot a term referring to a particular TV commercial, usually in its "encoded" or computer form, and known by a "spot identifier" code, permitting that commercial to be referenced in a schedule or in a log. A typical spot is 30 seconds in length.

Spot ID a code name assigned by Traffic to a spot, permitting reference to that spot in schedules and logs. Once the spot has been encoded, the spot ID is used as the file name to enable storage, transport, and playback of that spot.

Spot-Log a record made by the inserter stating what spot it played, the network, the date and time, and the success or failure of the playback. These files were sent back from a leaf to the portal, from the portal to

HOME, and then were acquired by Traffic. The records enable billing of customers for the service of playing their spots as requested. (Obviously if a spot fails to play, they cannot be billed.)

State in the encyclicals and other "social teaching" documents, the highest, comprehensive social organization of humans: at times it can mean a country, its government, or the collective power of its citizens, in whatever form it may be arranged or formulated.

Subsidiarity [from a Latin military term meaning the third line of soldiers, who assist and support the principal lines.] The common-sense principle of order and right relation between members and groups of a human social group, or, by extension, any system of cooperating entities.

Subtree the collection of inserters at a given location: one inserter, called the Portal, can communicate with HOME by satellite; the others, called the leaves, can communicate with the portal by network.

System [from Greek roots meaning "placed together"] Broadly, any organised collection of entities, grouped together by some rational purpose or order; specifically, a collection of equipment, usually computers, working together to accomplish a task or solve a problem. Sometimes short for "Operating System." In anatomy, a collection of related organs, or parts of a living being which work together to perform their function, such as the circulatory system.

Tell-tale A signal light (or an equivalent symbol on a computer screen), usually of different colors, which indicates the status of some component of machinery, often distant from the place where the display is located.

To-Be-Encoded List The list of spots needed somewhere in the Field which are not yet stored in the MASTER LIBRARY; it is generated by PUMP and made visible to the Operations Department in the Control Room by WATCHER.

To-Be-Sent List The list of spots needed in somewhere in the Field which are in the MASTER LIBRARY and are to be sent by PUMP to the Portals requesting them; it is it is generated by PUMP and made visible to the Operations Department in the Control Room by WATCHER.

Traffic Department (also called Traffic) A department which performs the following tasks (1) receive tapes from customers and assign spot identifiers to them for scheduling (2) produce schedules which instruct the machinery as to what spots to play on what networks at what times and in what locations (3) process the logs returned from the Field which provide the information for billing of the customers.

Traffic and Billing A computer program used by the Traffic Department which (1) produces the schedules from requests made by customers, and (2) produces the bills from the logs returned from the Field.

Transport The delivery of files (primarily spots, schedules, and

120

logs) between the equipment at Headquarters and the equipment in the Field.

Tree In the branch of mathematics called graph theory, a tree is an abstract object based on a collection of entities called *nodes* which are related to each other in pairs as parent and child, subject to the following restrictions: (1) no node has more than one parent (2) only one node, called the *root*, has no parent (3) there is no *cycle* – a path linking a node back to itself (4) there is a path leading from every node to the root (the graph is *connected*). In computer science, a tree is a representation of a mathematical tree, usually stored within memory; there are a large variety of specialized forms, each of which have its own special properties and uses. One common form is the "hierarchical file system" in use on various operating systems, which has a directory called the *root* (written as "c:\"); it can contain files or sub-directories; the sub-directories can also contain files or sub-directories, and so on. (Yes, a file is a "leaf" within the directory tree.)

Vein A blood vessel within which blood flows *towards* the heart. (Though there is also a large blood vessel going from the digestive system to the liver which is called the *portal vein*; no pun intended.)

VSAT [Very Small Aperture Terminal] A bi-directional (two-way) communications technique by which communications from one geographical location to a number of wide-spread locations is made by means of a satellite.

VTR [Video Tape Recorder] A device similar to the VCR (Video Cassette Recorder) which plays back or records video and audio by means of magnetic media (tape). Such tapes are frequently protected within a larger or smaller plastic package (a cassette), and the terms are often interchangeable. For ad insertion, the major activity is playback, as this is an essential part of the encoding operation. In that operation, the VTR is actually controlled by a computer as the video and audio are converted to electronic forms.

WATCHER The computer program used by the Operations Department to perform monitoring. WATCHER is continuously visible in the Control Room and shows by colored dots ("tell-tales") the status of the various machines in the Field, as well as those of the Home Cluster; it also shows the current "To-Be-Encoded" and "To-Be-Sent" lists produced by PUMP.

Window In a schedule arranged by the Traffic department, an interval of time, typically an hour or more, which is specified for a given network, headend, and date, together with a list of spots for that window. If that network sends its triggering signal, or cue-tone, during that time on that date, the inserter at that headend will play those spots.

Bibliography

Note: All Bible quotes are from the Douay-Rheims version.

Anselm. *St. Anselm: Basic Writings*. Translated by S. N. Deane. (Open Court, La Salle, IL, 1903, 1962).

Aquinas, St. Thomas. *Summa Contra Gentiles*. Translated by Anton C. Pegis, F. R. S. C. (Notre Dame: University of Notre Dame Press, 1975).

—. *Summa Theologica*. Translated by Fathers of the English Dominican Province. (Allen, Texas: Christian Classics, 1948).

Arey, L.B. *Developmental Anatomy*. (Philadelphia: W. B. Saunders Co., 1965).

Bartlett, John. *Familiar Quotations*. (Boston: Little, Brown and Company, 1955).

Chesterton, G. K. *The Ball and the Cross* (in *Collected Works* Vol. 7: San Francisco: Ignatius Press, 2004).

—. *Charles Dickens* (in *Collected Works* Vol. 15: San Francisco: Ignatius Press, 1989).

—. *The Common Man* (New York: Sheed and Ward, 1950).

—. *The Everlasting Man* (in *Collected Works* Vol. 2: San Francisco: Ignatius Press, 1986).

—. *Heretics* (in *Collected Works* Vol. 1: San Francisco: Ignatius Press, 1986).

—. *Illustrated London News* (in *Collected Works* Vols. 27-35: San Francisco: Ignatius Press, 1986-91)

—. *The New Jerusalem* (in *Collected Works* Vol. 20: San Francisco: Ignatius Press, 2001).

—. *Orthodoxy* (in *Collected Works* Vol. 1: San Francisco: Ignatius Press, 1986).

—. *The Poet and the Lunatics*. (New York: Sheed and Ward, 1955).

—. *Robert Browning*. (New York: The Macmillan Company, 1903).

—. *St. Thomas Aquinas* (in *Collected Works* Vol. 2: San Francisco: Ignatius Press, 1986).

—. *The Secret of Father Brown* (in *Collected Works* Vol. 12: San Francisco: Ignatius Press, 2005).

—. *The Thing* (in *Collected Works* Vol. 3: San Francisco: Ignatius Press, 1990).

—. *Tremendous Trifles*. (New York: Sheed and Ward, 1955).

—. *What's Wrong With the World* (in *Collected Works* Vol. 4: San Francisco: Ignatius Press, 1987).

Cole, Rex Vicat. *The Artistic Anatomy of Trees*. (New York: Dover Publications, 1965).

Darnell, J., Lodish, H., and Baltimore, D. *Molecular Cell Biology*. (New York: Scientific American Books, 1990).

DiFiore, Mariano S. H. *Atlas of Human Histology*. (Philadelphia: Lea & Febiger, 3rd ed., 1967).

Grant, J. C. Boileau. *Grant's Atlas of Anatomy*. (Baltimore: The Williams & Wilkins Co. 1972).

Gray, Henry. *Gray's Anatomy*. (New York: Bounty Books, 1977).

Greisheimer, Esther M. *Physiology and Anatomy*. (Philadelphia: J. B. Lippincott Co., 1963).

Guyton, Arthur C. *Textbook of Medical Physiology*. (Philadelphia: W. B. Saunders Co., 1981).

Ham, Arthur Worth. *Histology*. (Philadelphia: J. B. Lippincott, 1957).

Hart, Charles A. *Thomistic Metaphysics*. (Englewood Cliffs, N.J.: Prentice-Hall,

1959).

Jaki, S. L. *Chesterton, A Seer of Science.* (Port Huron, MI: Real View Books, 2001).

—. *The Limits of a Limitless Science.* (Wilmington, DE: ISI Books, 2000).

—. *The Purpose of It All.* (Washington, D.C.: Regnery Gateway, 1990).

—. *Science and Creation.* (Edinburgh: Scottish Academic Press, 1986).

Juster, Norton. *The Phantom Tollbooth.* (New York: Random House, 1961).

John XXIII. *Mater et Magistra.* (1961).

—. *Pacem in Terris.* (1963).

John Paul II. *Centesimus Annus.* (1991).

—. *Laborem Exercens.* (1981).

Kimber, Diana C., Gray, Carolyn E., Stackpole, Caroline E., and Leavell, Lutie C. *Anatomy and Physiology.* (New York: The Macmillan Co. 1961).

Kreyche, Robert J. *First Philosophy.* (New York: Holt, Rhinehart and Winston, Inc., 1959).

Leo XIII. *Rerum Novarum.* (1891).

Lewis, Charlton T. and Short, Charles. *A Latin Dictionary.* (Oxford University Press, 1996).

Marchant, J. R. V. and Charles, J. F. *Cassell's Latin-English and English-Latin Dictionary.* (Toronto: Cassell and Co., 1910).

Martinez, Most Rev. Luis M. *The Sanctifier.* (Boston: Daughters of St. Paul, 1982).

McCollough, David. *The Great Bridge.* (New York: Touchstone: Simon & Schuster, 1972)

Morison, Samuel Eliot. *Admiral of the Ocean Sea.* (Boston: Little, Brown and Co., 1942)

Newman, John Henry Cardinal. *The Idea of a University.* (Garden City, NY: Image Books, 1959).

Patten, Bradley M. *Foundations of Embryology.* (New York: McGraw-Hill, 1964).

Pius XI. *Quadragesimo Anno* (1931).

Prümmer, Dominic M. *Handbook of Moral Theology.* (Roman Catholic Books, Ft. Collins, CO, 1957).

Sayers, Dorothy L. *The Mind of the Maker.* (New York: HarperCollins, 1941, 1968).

Shallo, Michael W. *Scholastic Philosophy.* (Philadelphia: The Peter Reilly Company, 1944).

Taylor, Jerome. *The Didascalicon of Hugh of St. Victor.* (New York and London: Columbia University Press, 1961).

Windle, Bertram C. A. *The Catholic Church and its Reactions with Science.* (New York: The Macmillan Co., 1927).

Code of Canon Law, Latin-English Edition. (Washington, D.C.: Canon Law Society of America, 1983).

Made in the USA
San Bernardino, CA
23 March 2013